T0346425

Monetary Policy Rules

STUDIEN ZUR INTERNATIONALEN WIRTSCHAFTSFORSCHUNG

Herausgegeben von
Ralf Fendel und André Schmidt

Band 1

PETER LANG

Frankfurt am Main · Berlin · Bern · Bruxelles · New York · Oxford · Wien

Dirk Bleich

Monetary Policy Rules

Empirical Applications Based on Survey Data

PETER LANG
Internationaler der Wissenschaften

Bibliographic Information published by the Deutsche Nationalbibliothek
The Deutsche Nationalbibliothek lists this publication in the Deutsche Nationalbibliografie; detailed bibliographic data is available in the internet at http://dnb.d-nb.de.

Zugl.: Vallendar, Wiss. Hochsch. für Unternehmensführung, Diss., 2011

Cover Design:
© Olaf Gloeckler, Atelier Platen, Friedberg

D 992
ISSN 1866-234X
ISBN 978-3-631-61658-1

© Peter Lang GmbH
Internationaler Verlag der Wissenschaften
Frankfurt am Main 2012
All rights reserved.

www.peterlang.de

For my family

Acknowledgment

The subsequent piece of work has been accepted as my dissertation thesis at the WHU - Otto Beisheim School of Management in Vallendar in May 2011. It would not have been possible to write it thesis without the help and support of the kind people around me. First and foremost, I would like to gratefully and sincerely thank Professor Michael Frenkel and Professor Ralf Fendel for their personal support, their thoughtful guidance, their great patience and their understanding at all times during my PhD studies at WHU - Otto Beisheim School of Management. Their mentorship was of immeasurable value for my personal development and, most importantly, their friendship was the basis for an incomparable and unique environment. Their support and understanding during the time my son Alexander was born surpassed everything I expected.

I am also indebted to many of my current and former colleagues and friends at the Department of Economics at the WHU. In particular, these are Tobias Biller, Niklas Gadatsch, Eliza Lis, Nicole Reufels, Dr. Günter Schmidt, Andreas Tudyka and Lilli Zimmermann. All of them have contributed significantly to this work. A special thank is directed to Professor Achim Czerny for his support in Mathematica. Moreover, I owe my deepest gratitude to Professor Jan-Christoph Rülke. Without his guidance and help this thesis could have hardly been accomplished.

I would like to acknowledge the financial, academic, and technical support of the WHU - Otto Beisheim School of Management and its staff. The library facilities, the computer facilities, and the administrative facilities have been indispensable.

I am grateful to my friend Ernst Borchert. Additionally, I would like to thank two friends I met during my PhD studies at the WHU. These are Frederick Krummet and Maximilian André Müller.

Without the constant support of my family this dissertation would have never been possible. I am endlessly grateful for what my parents have done for me. They were *always* accessible for me. Their unconditional love, their hard work, their financial support, and their self-sacrificing devotion are *the* foundation for who I am today and, thus, for writing this thesis. I would also like to express my deeply-felt thanks to my brother Torsten for his support, his advice, and his encouragement. Without him I would have never written this thesis. Finally, I would like to thank my wife and my son: "Uese" to Cynthia and Alexander Erhunmwunse.

Dirk Bleich   Frankfurt am Main, December 2011

Contents

List of Tables

List of Figures

Chapter 1

Introduction

As Taylor and Williams (2010) express, economist have been interested in monetary policy rules since the advent of economics. Adam Smith already suggested in the *Wealth of Nations* that a "well-regulated paper-money" is superior to a pure commodity standard in terms of fostering economic growth and stability. Other classical economists such as Henry Thornton and David Ricardo specified Smith's idea by stressing the importance of a rule-based monetary policy to avoid financial crises. Irving Fisher's *quantity theory of money* and Knut Wicksel's *interest theory* of the early 20th century can be considered as further cornerstones. In the 1960s, Milton Friedman revived the quantity theory of money and suggested his *constant growth rate rule*. Finally, Taylor (1993) introduced a monetary policy rule, which relates the short-term interest rate to deviations of inflation and output from their respective target levels. This rule became generally known as the Taylor rule.

Since the seminal work of Taylor (1993), different variants of Taylor rules – often labeled Taylor type rules – have been developed. In particular, Clarida et al. (1998) proposed a specific forward-looking variant of the Taylor rule which takes into account account the pre-emptive nature of monetary policy as well as interest smoothing behavior of central banks. This type of reaction function has become very popular in applied research and also will be in the center of this thesis. For evaluation of monetary policy the resulting reaction coefficient for the inflation rate is of particular interest. If the central bank adjusts its nominal policy rate by more than one-for-one with the inflation rate, the real interest rate will increase and thus monetary policy is inflation stabilizing. A central bank that acts in such a manner is often referred to fulfill the so-called *Taylor principle*. If the Taylor principle does not hold, the central bank reaction leads to declining real interest rates in the case of rising inflation, which clearly is at odds with stabilizing efforts.[1] This discussion already gives an intuitive explanation of why the fulfillment of the Taylor principle is associated with an inflation stabilizing policy. The *theoretical* derivation of the Taylor principle is based on the consideration of stability conditions of economic equilibrium in a specific economic model. The question of interest is whether a monetary policy rule will lead to stable equilibrium. If a monetary policy rule does not lead to a stable equilibrium, it can be considered as undesirable, because it cannot be assumed that economic agents will co-ordinate on that equilibrium.

The aim of this thesis is to provide different studies of how econometric evaluation of monetary policy based on forward-looking Taylor rules is conducted. As will be demonstrated, such a relatively simple monetary policy rule is well suited to analyze a wide range of questions regarding monetary policy.[2] This thesis provides three different applications including how the introduction of inflation targeting affects monetary policy, the role of oil price expectations for monetary policy, and how monetary policy is associated to developments in the housing sector. Based on these studies the thesis derives two main results: First, forward-looking Taylor-type rules are well suited to be applied to the real world and, second, macroeconomic performance has been better when central bank decisions are based on such rules.[3]

For empirical application this thesis uses survey data about expectations provided by Consensus Economics. There are several reasons why this data set is in particular suitable for the purpose of this thesis. The main advantage is that the forecasts are currently observed data which are not revised and, hence not exposed to the *real-time data critique* by Orphanides (2001). Another important advantage is that the data set is consistent across countries and time periods. This feature makes the data set in particular suitable for panel data studies. Further advantages will be discussed in the subsequent chapters.

This thesis is structured as follows: Chapter 2 gives a comprehensive treatment for the derivation of the stability conditions for a forward-looking Taylor rule in the basic New Keynesian model, which has become the workhorse for the analysis of monetary policy in recent years (Galí, 2008).

---

[1]   Note that the reaction to the output gap is also of importance. Details will be discussed in Chapter 2.

[2]   This is a fairly general result that was demonstarted in many other studies before.

[3]   Note that Taylor and Williams (2010) come to the same conclusion.

As already stated above, the utilization of forward-looking policy rules requires the usage of expectational data. As Rülke (2009) discusses, there is an ongoing debate of how expectations are formed and in particular whether individuals are fully rational when forming expectations about the future. Although several econometric studies suggest that individuals are not fully rational, it is still standard to assume rational expectations in economic theory. To address the issue of bounded rationality, this thesis considers the econometric learning approach (Evans and Honkapohja, 2001) as an alternative to the rational expectation hypothesis. This alternative approach has become very famous in recent years and assumes that economic agents minimally deviate from rational expectations in a sense that expectations are based on a learning process. As Bullard and Mitra (2002) demonstrate this alternative assumption alters stability conditions. However, under both assumptions the fulfillment of the Taylor principle is strongly associated with the stability of the model's equilibrium. This chapter's result will allow for a meaningful evaluation of the subsequent empirical studies in Chapter 3, Chapter 4 and Chapter 5, which focus on the application of forward-looking Taylor type rules.

Chapter 3 focuses on the question whether the introduction of inflation targeting changes central banks' monetary policy reaction functions towards a higher weight on inflation stabilizing. Although Svensson (1997, 2003) provides theoretical evidence that the introduction of inflation targeting is consistent with a monetary policy aiming to stabilizing inflation, empirical evidence is still missing. Chapter 3 aims to close this gap and considers 18 inflation targeting countries before and after the introduction of inflation targeting. The chapter's result gives strong empirical evidence that the introduction of inflation targeting is associated with am inflation stabilizing monetary policy.

Chapter 4 investigates the consequences of oil price movements for monetary policy. The debate on whether central banks should respond to the oil price is remarkable but contentious (Bernanke et al., 1997, Hamilton and Herrera 2004, Blanchard and Gali 2007, Svensson 2006). However, there is no study examining whether central banks actually respond to the oil price. This chapter addresses this issue by estimating oil price augmented monetary policy reaction functions. Since this thesis tries to capture the preemptive nature of monetary policy by estimating *forward-looking* reaction functions, an oil price augmented forward-looking Taylor rule should include oil price *expectations* rather than the actual oil price. Again, the Consensus Economics data set, which also includes expectations on the oil price, seems to be in particular suitable for this purpose. Following this approach, this chapter provides robust estimates that the Bank of Canada, Bank of England, Federal Reserve and the European Central Bank respond to increases in oil price expectations with an increase in the interest rate. Interestingly, these central banks do not respond to the realized oil price.

In a first step, Chapter 5 analyzes monetary policy conditions in Spain before and after the changeover to the Euro by estimating forward-looking Taylor-type rules. Based on the Taylor principle, the ECB's monetary policy since 1999 can be evaluated as too expansionary for Spain's economy. In a second step, these findings are linked to the developments in the Spanish housing sector. This chapter provides evidence that the Spanish housing boom and the subsequent burst of the housing bubble is associated with the ECB's "one-size-fits-all" monetary policy. Consequently, this chapter's analysis serves as a prime example for an asymmetric monetary policy effect in a monetary union. Finally, Chapter 6 concludes the main results of this thesis.

Chapter 2

Stability conditions for forward-looking monetary policy rules in the basic New Keynesian model

2.1 Introduction

Since the seminal paper of Taylor (1993) it has virtually become a convention to describe the interest rate setting behavior of central banks in terms of monetary policy reaction functions. In its plain form, the so-called Taylor rule states that the short-term interest rate, i.e., the instrument of a central bank, reacts to deviations of inflation and output from their respective target levels. For the purpose of econometric analysis the original Taylor rule has been modified in several ways. One important modification is the usage of *forward-looking* instead of *contemporaneous* data. The theoretical justification for this is that monetary policy works with a lag and, thus, effective monetary policy should focus on *forecast* values of the goal variables, rather than the current values. Among others, Clarida et al. (1998) and Taylor (1999) show that central banks in deed act in a forward-looking manner.

For evaluation of monetary policy, it is of particular importance how the interest rate reacts to deviations of the inflation rate from its target level. In order to act in a stabilizing manner the central bank has to react with its nominal policy rate more than proportional to underlying inflation shocks.

This will result in an increase of the real interest rate.[1] Such an inflation stabilizing policy is often referred to as the well known *Taylor principle*. If the Taylor principle does not hold, the central bank reaction leads to declining real interest rates in the case of rising inflation which clearly is at odds with stabilizing efforts.

This discussion already gives an intuitive explanation of why the fulfillment of the Taylor principle is associated with an inflation stabilizing policy. However, the Taylor principle can also be derived theoretically by considering stability conditions of economic equilibrium. Since the so-called *basic New Keynesian model* has become the workhorse for the analysis of monetary policy in recent years (Galí, 2008), this model will also be used in this chapter. The most important features of this model are the micro-founded forward-looking character, the assumption of imperfect competition in the goods market, and the constraints in the sense of Calvo (1983) on the frequency with which firms can adjust their prices. A fundamental result for this class of models is that monetary policy is non-neutral (Galí, 2008). That is, the equilibrium path of the real variables cannot be determined independently of a monetary policy rule, which governs how the nominal interest rate evolves over time. An important issue in this regard is whether the monetary policy rule will lead to a stable equilibrium (Bullard and Mitra, 2002). If a monetary policy rule does not lead to a stable equilibrium it can be considered as undesirable because it cannot be assumed that economic agents will coordinate on that equilibrium. The possibility for unstable outcomes is due to private sector expectations that enter such a model explicitly. More precisely, current economic variables depend on their future expectations, which in turn depend on current economic variables. This interdependent (or self-referential) character is crucial for the path of the economy and thus for stability.

The standard approach for modeling expectations is to assume *rational expectations* (RE), which was first explicitly formulated by Muth (1961). In general, monetary policy rules should be designed in a way that an equilibrium under RE, also called *rational expectations equilibrium* (REE), is determinate. Determinacy means that the REE is locally unique and therefore there do not exist any other nearby REE. In the case of indeterminacy the system is expected to be highly volatile and thus not desirable.

As shown by Clarida et al. (2000) the study of determinacy is highly relevant for the conduct of practical monetary policy. Before the appointment

---

[1]   Note that the reaction to the output gap is also of importance. Details will be dis-
       cussed below.

of Paul Volker as a Federal Reserve Chairman in 1979, U.S. inflation in the 1960s and 1970s was high and volatile. More precisely, they estimate forward-looking Taylor rules and find that the Taylor principle does not hold for the pre-Volker era. Analytically, this period corresponds to an indeterminate REE. In contrast, the low and stable inflation rates since 1979 coincides with a determinate REE, which roughly means that the Taylor principle is fulfilled.

Due to the importance of the Taylor principle for empirical analysis and practical monetary policy, in this chapter we would like to give a comprehensive treatment for the derivation of the Taylor principle for a forward-looking Taylor rule, i.e. the conditions for a stable REE in the basic New Keynesian Model. Moreover, we introduce the adaptive (or econometric) learning approach (Evans and Honkapohja, 2001) as an alternative to the strong RE hypothesis.[2] However, despite the strong RE assumption, results based on RE can be considered as an important benchmark. This approach has received increasing attention among the economic community in recent years and assumes that economic agents deviate minimally from RE in the sense that economic agents are to be about as smart as (good) economists, who behave like econometricians or statisticians when forecasting future variables of the economy (Evans and Honkapohja, 2009). This assumption allows for forecast errors and a misspecified forecasting model. Especially after exogenous structural changes in the economy it cannot be assumed that economic agents will immediately evaluate all relevant information in a way consistent with RE. However, it is of interest to study whether the the REE can be reached over time, if economists engage in a learning process. This is, they reestimate and reformulate the model as new data becomes available. In other words, will the economy converge over time to the (unique) REE when expectations are based on the adaptive learning approach. Moreover, if the REE is indeterminate and there are multiple equilibria under RE, the learning approach can serve as a selection criterion. This is the case if only one of the equlilibria under RE includes learnability.

This chapter has the following structure. Section 2.2 introduces the basic New Keynesian model. In Section 2.3 we introduce the idea of equilibrium

---

[2]   The RE assumption is very strong, because it postulates that economic agents have a great deal of knowledge in the sense that they possess all relevant information and are able to evaluate this information without systematic mistakes. For example, even in relatively simple models with constant expectations, the RE hypothesis requires the full knowledge of the structure of the model, the values of the parameters and that the random shocks are identically and independently distributed.

and show the conditions for stability of economic equilibrium under rational expectations. Then we derive the Taylor principle for a forward-locking
Taylor rule under rational expectations (Section 2.3.3) and under adaptive
learning (Section 2.4).[3] Finally, Section 2.5 concludes.

2.2   The basic New Keynesian model

The basic New Keynesian model can be represented in terms of two equations.[4] The first equation is called *dynamic IS (DIS) equation* and describes
the demand side of the economy:

$$(2.1)\qquad\qquad x_t = -\varphi\left(i_t - E_t^*\pi_{t+1}\right) + E_t^* x_{t+1} + g_t.$$

The output gap, x_t, depends negatively on the real interest rate given by
the difference of the nominal interest rate and the forward-looking inflation
rate, $i_t - E_t^*\pi_{t+1}$, and positively on the forward-looking output gap, $E_t x_{t+1}$.
Equation (2.1) can be obtained the following way: First, an Euler equation is
derived by maximizing household's lifetime utility with respect to its budget
constraint. This Euler equation is then log-linearized. Under the usage of the
market clearing condition, $y_t = c_t$ ((log-)output equals (log-)consumption),
and moreover, rewriting this in terms of the the output gap, one finally arrives
at the DIS equation.

The main difference in comparison to the traditional IS curve is the
forward-looking character of (2.1): Output not only depends on the interest
rate, but also on the the expected future output. For example, a higher expected future output increases the individual's wealth over lifetime. Because
individuals are assumed to be forward-looking and also to prefer to smooth
their consumption over time, they will use a fraction of the additional wealth
for increasing today's consumption. Since output is demand side determined
in the New Keynesian setup,[5] a higher current output will be reached. The
parameter φ is strictly positive and a measure for the intertemporal elasticity
of substitution. A higher value indicates that the representative household

---

[3]   Please note that this problem was first considered by Bullard and Mitra (2002). The
      results presented in this chapter are based on their article.

[4]   For a detailed comprehensive treatment see, for example, Galí (2008) and Woodford
      (2003).

[5]   Due to the assumption of monopolistic competition, firms are able to set prices above
      their marginal costs, which allows them to satisfy demand.

is *more* willing to allow its consumption to vary over time, and therefore, the same rise in the real interest rate leads to stronger decline in the output gap.[6] Finally, g_t describes a demand shock that will be specified below.

The second equation is labeled *New Keynesian Phillips Curve* (NKPC) and describes the supply side of the economy:

$$(2.2) \qquad \pi_t = \beta E_t^* \pi_{t+1} + \kappa x_t + u_t.$$

The current inflation rate, π_t, depends positively on the forward-looking inflation rate, on the output gap, and a supply shock, u_t. The parameter β is the household's discount factor and satisfies $0 < \beta < 1$; κ is assumed to be strictly positive.

For the derivation of the NKPC it is assumed that firms operate in an environment of monopolistic competition. In addition to that, firms face constraints on the frequency with which they can adjust their prices. More precisely Calvo (1983) pricing is assumed. That is, producers can reset the prices of their goods in each period with a probability of $1 - \theta$, where θ is an index for the degree of price stickiness that needs to satisfy the condition $0 \leq \theta < 1$. As a consequence, each producer sets its price to maximize current and future profits taking into account the average time over which prices are fixed.

An explicit derivation of equation (2.2) shows that the coefficient κ is decreasing in θ. However, for the sake of brevity we here restrict to a short intuitive explanation: A higher θ implies that prices are fixed for a longer time on average. Therefore, changes in the output gap due to demand variations will cause a less sensitive response of inflation. At this point, we would like to point out the forward-looking character of (2.2): Inflation depends entirely on current and expected future economic variables. Thus in contrast to the traditional Phillips curve, there is no lagged dependence on inflation.

The shocks, g_t and u_t, are assumed to follow first-order autoregressive processes and are given by

$$(2.3) \qquad g_t = \mu g_{t-1} + \tilde{g}_t,$$

$$(2.4) \qquad u_t = \rho u_{t-1} + \tilde{u}_t,$$

---

[6]   To avoid confusion we note that some authors use the reciprocal value for φ. This would imply that for a higher value of φ the representative household is *less* willing to allow its consumption to vary over time.

where $0 \leq \mu < 1$ and $0 \leq \rho < 1$, and where both $\tilde{g}_t$ and $\tilde{u}_t$ are i.i.d. white noise shocks with variance σ_g^2 and σ_u^2, respectively.

Note that the expectation operator in (2.1) and (2.2) is marked with an asterisk. This indicates that the expectations need not be rational. Whenever writing the expectation operator without an asterisk we have RE.

As already stated above, monetary policy in the (basic) New Keynesian Model is non-neutral and has to be supplemented by a monetary policy rule. This monetary policy rules governs how the nominal interest rate evolves over time. As already stated above, we will restrict this chapter's analysis to a forward-looking Taylor rule.

2.3 Stability of equilibrium under rational expectations

2.3.1 The idea of equilibrium

The model introduced in the previous section is classified as a *dynamic stochastic general equilibrium model* (DSGE model in short). This class of models has become standard in macroeconomics in recent years. It is *dynamic* because of the intertemporal approach and *stochastic* because of the exogenous components given by (2.3) and (2.4). For the analysis of equilibrium it is important to understand what is meant by *general equilibrium*.

General equilibrium models use individual markets and agents as a basis to built up the economy. This idea goes back to Walras (1874). Broadly speaking, an auctioneer will announce prices for the different type of goods of the economy. For the announced prices of the goods each individual has to tell how much it would sell or buy. As long as demand and supply in the different markets do not match, the auctioneer continues to announce prices. Prices for goods with excess demand will be raised and prices with excess demand will be lowered. Once supply equals demand in all markets transaction take place. The equilibrium is then given by a vector of prices and a vector of goods. However, it cannot be taken for granted that an equilibrium exist or that economic agents are able to co-ordinate on an equilibrium.

Traditionally, general equilibrium theory has been used in microeconomics. In contrast, the first macroeconomic models such as Keynes' (1936) *General*

Theory can be classified as *partial equilibrium* theory. It considers large aggregates that are assumed rather than derived. Market clearing of a specific good does not depend on prices and quantities demanded and supplied in other markets. The lack of an explicit derivation of aggregate relationships was subject to heavy criticism among several economists. As a consequence, economists started to derive aggregates from a microeconomic foundation and thus general equilibrium theory found its way into modern macroeconomics.

Referring to the basic New Keynesian model introduced in Section 2.2 the character of a general equilibrium model is due to the following assumptions: As already stated above, equation (2.1) is obtained by maximizing the (intertemporal) utility of a representative household. More precisely the representative household has to decide (i) about the optimal combination of individual goods and (ii) about the level of total consumption which includes the decision about the amount of work to be supplied. Equation (2.2) is the outcome of maximizing the (intertemporal) profits of individual firms. Thus one has to bear in mind that the aggregate equations (2.1) and (2.2) are due to a microeconomic foundation that describe the optimal behavior of individuals. This is what makes the model to be classified as a general equilibrium model.

2.3.2 How economics differ from natural science: The role of expectations

In Section 2.2 we already pointed out the forward-looking character of the basic New Keynesian model. It is important to be aware of the consequences of this attribute, namely that the current state of the economy depends on the beliefs of human beings about the future. Moreover, these beliefs in turn depend on current economic variables. In this regard economics (or social science in general) differs clearly from natural science where beliefs about the future do not enter. As Farmer (1999) states, this difference is crucial for the path of the economy and thus for study of stability of equilibrium.

In this section we will assume expectations to be rational. The idea of rational expectations (RE) was first explicitly formulated by Muth (1961) and became very influential due to the work of Lucas (1976). He states that policy-invariant econometric models will not be successful in forecasting future variables if economic agents have rational expectations. More precisely, the effects of a change in a particular policy cannot be predicted correctly by a model with parameters that do not account for the possibility of a policy change. Thus using such a model is equivalent to extrapolating the past to the future, which is called *adaptive expectations* (and should not be confused with adaptive learning). The problem with adaptive expectations is that it leaves out important available information (for example an observable policy change). Of course only rational individuals will be able to predict the consequences of a policy change in a correct way.

Rational expectations imply that economic agents possess all relevant information and are able to evaluate this information without systematic mistakes. In fact this is a quite strong assumption. For example, it requires the full knowledge of the structure of the model, the values of the parameters and that the random shocks are identically and independently distributed. Although these strong assumptions have been criticized, the RE assumption is standard when formulating future beliefs of individuals in economic models. In this sense results based on RE can be considered as an important benchmark.

The study of stability of equilibrium of a DSGE model that incorporates RE requires special techniques that are exclusively applied in economics. In the next subsection we will give a general introduction to these techniques for (log-)linear models. Moreover, we will demonstrate how these techniques are applied to the basic New Keynesian model with a forward-locking Taylor rule.

2.3.3   Determinacy as an important property of equilibrium

An important issue regarding general equilibrium analysis is the question under which conditions an equilibrium is determinate. Determinacy means that an equilibrium is locally isolated (locally unique). It implies that after the occurrence of an exogenous shock the model's state variables will always have the tendency to move back to the *same* equilibrium point. In case of indeterminacy it cannot be said where the state variables will settle down after an exogenous shock. It *can* be the case that over time the old equilibrium will be reached again. But there exists also the possibility that no or an adjacent equilibrium will be reached. Models that generate multiple equilibria are often considered as not very useful, because (without any additional criteria) there is nothing that can be said about the steady state of the economy. Thus the property of determinacy can be considered as a basic requirement that a model should satisfy.[7]

For the analysis of determinacy one needs to solve linear difference rational expectation models. To do so, we use techniques suggested by Blanchard and Kahn (1980) and, moreover, follow Farmer's (1999) methodology to some extent. We start with a model given by

$$
(2.5) \qquad \begin{bmatrix} Y_t^1 \\ Y_t^2 \end{bmatrix} = A \begin{bmatrix} Y_{t+1}^1 \\ Y_{t+1}^2 \end{bmatrix} + FZ_t, \qquad Y_{t=0}^1 = Y_0,
$$

where Y_t^1 (Y_t^2) is a vector of dimension n_1 (n_2) and Z_t is a vector of dimension k. The vector $Y_t = [Y_t^1, Y_t^2]'$ has a dimension of $n = n_1 + n_2$. The matrix A has the dimension $n \times n$ and contains all intertemporal linkage of the model. F is a $n \times k$ matrix not further specified. Z_t includes exogenous variables that are assumed to follow first-order AR-processes (such as (2.3) or (2.4) for example). The variables included in Y_t are called *state variables* and give a complete description of the economy at date t. All other variables of interest can be expressed as functions of these state variables. Thus the behavior of Y_t is of interest. More precisely, we are interested whether Y_t will converge to a equilibrium that is (locally) unique.

We now turn to a point that is of crucial importance for the study of linear difference rational expectation models. The vector of state variables can include *predetermined* variables, Y_t^1, or *non-predetermined* (also known as *jump* or *free*) variables, Y_t^2. We follow definitions of Buiter (1982) to make clear the difference between predetermined and non-predetermined variables:

Definition 1: *Predetermined Variable*

$y_t^{1,i}$ *is a predetermined variable i.f.f.* $y_t^{1,i}$ *is not a function of expectations formed at date t, of future endogenous and/or exogenous variables.*

Here $y_t^{1,i}$ describes a variable that is an arbitrary element in the vector Y_t^1. An example often used for a predetermined variable is the capital stock. Its value depends only on variables that are determined one period before. As a consequence, predetermined variables have to be associated with an initial condition. This is why we need $Y_{t=0}^1 = Y_0$ in equation (2.5).

---

[7] However, in the case of indeterminacy it is possible to use the learning approach as a selection criterion. We will refer to this issue in Section 2.4

Definition 2: *Non-predetermined Variable*

$y_t^{2,i}$ *is a non-predetermined variable i.f.f.* $y_t^{2,i}$ *is a function of expectations formed at date t, of future endogenous and/or exogenous variables.*

Here $y_t^{2,i}$ describes a variable that is an arbitrary element the vector Y_t^2. An example for a non-predetermined variable is the inflation rate. Changes in beliefs of human beings about the future (e.g. a change in the expected inflation rate) will already change the value of the current inflation rate.

As Blanchard and Khan demonstrate, one has to relate the number of non-predetermined variables to the number eigenvalues of matrix A that are inside the unit circle.[8]

Theorem 1:

If the number of eigenvalues of matrix A inside the unit circle is equal to the number of non-predetermined variables, then the rational expectation equilibrium is unique.

Theorem 2:

If the number of eigenvalues of matrix A inside the unit circle exceeds the number of non-predetermined variables, then a stationary rational expectation equilibrium does not exists.

Theorem 3:

If the number of eigenvalues of matrix A inside the unit circle is less than the number of non-predetermined variables, then there are infinitely rational expectation equilibria

---

[8]   Blanchard and Kahn originally compared the number of non-predetermined variables to the number eigenvalues of A that are *outside* the unit circle. This is because they write the vector of forward looking state variables on the left hand side and the vector of current state variables on the right hand side of their system of difference equations. Because most of the literature we will refer to does not follow Blanchard and Kahn, it will turn out to be useful to write the system of difference equation in the form given by Equation (2.5).

As a result, a rational expectation equilibrium will only be determinate if proposition 1 holds.[9] For the reader who is interested in a formal proof of proposition 1 we refer to the article of Blanchard and Kahn. Instead we provide an intuitive explanation here. For this purpose we introduce a non-stochastic linear difference equation of the form

$$(2.6) \qquad z_{t+1} = \left(\frac{1}{a}\right) z_t.$$

In the case z_t in equation (2.6) describes a predetermined variable, the value of period $t+1$ depends on the value of period t (see definition 1). If we have the initial condition $z_{t=0} = z_0$, then, in period 1, z_1 is given by

$$(2.7) \qquad z_1 = \left(\frac{1}{a}\right) z_0,$$

in period 2

$$(2.8) \qquad z_2 = \left(\frac{1}{a}\right)^2 z_0,$$

and in period t

$$(2.9) \qquad z_t = \left(\frac{1}{a}\right)^t z_0.$$

From (2.9) it can be easily seen that z_t converges if $|a| > 1$.

However, if we assume z_t to be a non-predetermined variable the interpretation of (2.6) is different. According to definition 2 the value of period t now depends on the value of $t + 1$. In other words, what determines the current state of the variable are the expectations about the future of this variable and not its past values. Thus the direction how to solve equation (2.6) has to be reversed. If we iterate this equation into the future we obtain

$$(2.10) \qquad z_t = a^T z_{t+T}.$$

This equation converges if $|a| < 1$. As a result one can say that the direction in which a difference equation has to be solved – depending on

---

[9] Note that (global) uniqueness of course includes determinacy of equilibrium. In fact, in linear models local uniqueness (that is determinacy) will always include global uniqueness.

whether its state variable is predetermined or non-predetermined – governs the condition under which this difference equation is either stable or unstable.

Writing (2.6) in form of (2.5) we can interpret a to be the matrix A with a dimension of $n = 1$. As a consequence, *the* eigenvalue of A is given by a. If we now assume z_t to be a non-predetermined variable, we require a to be inside the unit circle for a unique equilibrium, that is $|a| < 1$. However if z_t is assumed to be a predetermined variable, a must lie outside the unit circle which is equivalent to $|a| > 1$.

This relatively simple illustration, of course, cannot be transfered one-to-one to the more complicated linear difference rational expectation models. However, we think that the relation between the number of non-predetermined variables and eigenvalues inside the unit circle suggested in proposition 1 is now intuitively tractable.

2.3.4 Deriving the Taylor principle for a forward-looking Taylor rule under rational expectations

We now use the previous subsection's results to derive the conditions for determinacy of a forward-looking Taylor rule given by[10]

(2.11) $i_t = \phi_\pi E_t \pi_{t+1} + \phi_x E_t x_{t+1}.$

The nominal interest rate, i_t, depends on the forward-looking inflation rate, $E_t \pi_{t+1}$, and the forward-looking output gap, $E_t x_{t+1}$. Expectations are assumed to be rational. As we will show now, the values of the parameters ϕ_π and ϕ_x play a crucial rule for determinacy. We here assume that both ϕ_π and ϕ_x are non-negative. Note that on the right hand side of (2.11) a constant term could be added. This way the central bank could make the interest rate rule consistent with a steady state value of zero for the inflation rate. Here we suppress the possibility of an intercept, because it is not relevant for the study of determinacy.

Inserting equation (2.11) into the DIS equation (2.1) and also using the NKPC (2.2), we can obtain the following system of difference equations:

(2.12) $A_1 \begin{bmatrix} x_t \\ \pi_t \end{bmatrix} = A_2 \begin{bmatrix} E_t x_{t+1} \\ E_t \pi_{t+1} \end{bmatrix} + \mathbf{v}_t,$

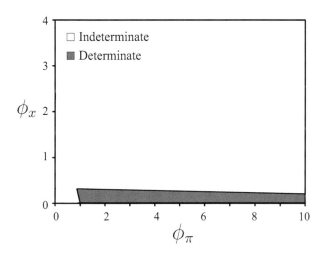

Figure 2.1: Determinacy for a forward-looking Taylor rule

Note: Figure 2.1 shows determinacy regions for combinations of ϕ_π and ϕ_x with calibration values of $\beta = 0.99$, $\kappa = 0.024$, $\varphi = \frac{1}{0.157}$ according to Woodford (1999).

where $A_1 = \begin{bmatrix} 1 & 0 \\ -\kappa & 1 \end{bmatrix}$, $A_2 = \begin{bmatrix} -\varphi\phi_x + 1 & \varphi(1 - \phi_\pi) \\ 0 & \beta \end{bmatrix}$, and $\mathbf{v}_t = \begin{bmatrix} g_t \\ u_t \end{bmatrix}$.

To obtain the conditions for determinacy we use the methods introduced in the previous subsection and obtain[11]

$$(2.13) \qquad \phi_x < \varphi^{-1}(1 + \beta^{-1}),$$

$$(2.14) \qquad \kappa(\phi_\pi - 1) + (1 - \beta)\phi_x < 2\varphi^{-1}(1 + \beta),$$

and

$$(2.15) \qquad \kappa(\phi_\pi - 1) + (1 + \beta)\phi_x > 0.$$

Thus we arrive at the following proposition:

Proposition 1:

---

[10]   The results are taken from Bullard and Mitra (2002).
[11]   For a detailed proof see Appendix A.

Under an interest rate rule of the type (2.11) *with forward-looking data the necessary and sufficient conditions for a REE to be unique are given by* (2.13), (2.14), *and* (2.15).

With $\phi_x = 0$ condition (2.15) requires $\phi_\pi > 1$. This is known as the Taylor (1993) principle. It states that the nominal interest rate has to respond by more than one-for-one to the inflation rate in order to achieve a rise in the real interest rate. If the central bank also puts some weight on the output gap, $\phi_\pi \leq 1$ can still lead to a determinate equilibrium. However, condition (2.15) is not sufficient for determinacy. Conditions (2.13) and (2.14) rule out too large values of ϕ_π and ϕ_x. If we use for example Woodford's (1999) calibration with $\beta = 0.99$, $\kappa = 0.024$, $\varphi = \frac{1}{0.157}$[12], determinacy occurs (roughly) for values of $\phi_x < 0.3156$ and $1 < \phi_\pi < 26,04$. Figure 2.1 gives an illustration for the region of determinacy.

We would like to point out that this calibration allows only for relatively low values of ϕ_x and would be at odds with several empirical studies. For example Clarida et al. (2000) obtain values of up to 1 for ϕ_x in time periods with low and relatively involatile inflation. However, with an alternative calibration suggested by Clarida et al. (2000) with values of $\beta = 0.99$, $\kappa = 0.3$, $\varphi = 1$, determinacy (roughly) occurs for values between 1 and 13 for ϕ_π and values of less than 2 for ϕ_x.

2.4 Adaptive Learning

In the previous section we considered the forward-looking Taylor rule (2.11) in the basic New Keynesian model under the assumption of RE. The results can only be expected to hold as long as the RE assumption holds, i.e. expectations about the future are consistent with actual outcomes, except for unforecastable random shocks. As argued by Evans and Honkapohja (2001) this strong assumption is implausible for reality. Instead of assuming perfect foresight of economic agents it seems more plausible that they initially do not have full knowledge about the economy. A quite realistic approach to model the behavior of economic agents is to assume that they behave like econometricians or statisticians when forecasting future variables. Following this approach, economic agents formulate and estimate a model, which they *perceive* to be correct. As new data becomes available they re-estimate and

---

[12]   This calibration is also used in Bullard and Mitra (2002).

possibly modify the model. In other words, economic agents *learn* about the economy. An important question is whether results based on RE will still hold if economic agents deviate minimally from RE as assumed by the adaptive learning approach. Determinacy remains an important benchmark, but it is not sufficient. The adaptive learning approach serves as an additional criterion for stability analysis. Moreover, the adaptive learning approach can be used in the case of multiple equilibria under RE (see proposition 3) as a selection criterion to single out a unique equilibrium.

2.4.1 The E-stability condition

In this subsection we develop the expectional stability (or E-stability) principle, which is closely linked to the adaptive learning approach.[13] To do so, we follow Evans and Honkapohja (2001). We start with a reduced form model, which can be obtained from demand and supply equations of the cobweb model:

$$(2.16) \qquad p_t = \mu + \alpha E_{t-1} p_t + \delta' w_{t-1} + \eta_t,$$

where p_t is the price in period t, $E_{t-1} p_t$ gives the RE of period $t-1$ for the price in period t, w_{t-1} is a vector of observable shocks with $E w_t = 0$ and unconditional second moment matrix $E w_t w_t' = \Omega$. The term η_t describes an i.i.d. white noise shocks with variance σ_η^2. Because $p_t = E_{t-1} p_t + \eta$ the unique rational expectation equilibrium (REE) is given by

$$(2.17) \qquad p_t = \bar{a} + \bar{b}' w_{t-1} + \eta_t,$$

where $\bar{a} = (1-\alpha)^{-1}\eta$ and $\bar{b} = (1-\alpha)^{-1}\delta$.[14]

We now use the adaptive learning approach as an additional criterion for stability analysis. We will show that the REE given by (2.17) will only be learnable under certain conditions, namely $\alpha < 1$. We assume that economic agents *perceive* the model

$$(2.18) \qquad p_t = a + b' w_{t-1} + \eta_t,$$

---

[13] Please note that this subsection is quite technical and demanding since it involes the analysis of convergence of least squares learning. The reader who is solely interested in the results of the stability conditions for a forward-looking Taylor Rule under adaptive learning might skip this subsection and directly move to Subsection 2.4.2.

[14] Note that the reason for the REE to be unique is that the current price, p_t, does not depend on expected future prices.

as a correct description. Equation (2.18) is called the *perceived law of motion* (PLM) and in this case it is structural identical to the REE given by (2.17). The unknown parameters a and b, however, can differ from $\bar{a}$ and $\bar{b}$. Since the adaptive learning approach assumes economic agents to act like econometricians or statisticians the parameter values of (2.18) are estimated by recursive least squares (RLS) from past data $\{p_i, w_i\}_{i=0}^{t-1}$. Note that the RLS estimator is a recursive form of the OLS estimator. According to the PLM (2.18) the forecast for p_t is then given by

$$(2.19) \qquad\qquad E_{t-1}^* p_t = a_{t-1} + b_{t-1}' w_{t-1},$$

where a_{t-1} and b_{t-1} denote the RLS estimator of the parameters. Inserting the forecast (2.19) into (2.16) gives a temporary equilibrium for period t of the form

$$(2.20) \qquad\qquad p_t = (\mu + \alpha a_{t-1}) + (\delta + \alpha b_{t-1})' w_{t-1} + \eta_t.$$

This temporary equilibrium is called the *actual law of motion* (ALM) and describes the stochastic process that the economy follows if economic agents base their forecast on a model given by the PLM. Every period – if new data becomes available – economic agents re-estimate the model. The question of interest is whether $a_t \to \bar{a}$ and $b_t \to \bar{b}$ as $t \to \infty$, i.e will the parameter values under adaptive learning converge to the values that are obtained under RE as time progresses.

At this point it turns out to be useful to define a *mapping* from the PLM (2.18) to the ALM (2.20) given by

$$(2.21) \qquad\qquad T\begin{pmatrix} a \\ b \end{pmatrix} = \begin{pmatrix} \mu + \alpha a \\ \delta + \alpha b \end{pmatrix}.$$

As a result the ALM (2.20) can be written as

$$(2.22) \qquad\qquad p_t = T(\phi_{t-1}) z_{t-1} + \eta_t.$$

where $\phi_t' = \begin{pmatrix} a_t & b_t' \end{pmatrix}$ and $z_i' = \begin{pmatrix} 1 & w_i' \end{pmatrix}$.

The RLS estimator is formally given by the two following equations

$$(2.23) \qquad \phi_t = \phi_{t-1} + t^{-1} R_t^{-1} z_{t-1} (z_{t-1}'(T(\phi_t - 1) - \phi_{t-1}) + \eta_t),$$

$$(2.24) \qquad\qquad R_t = R_{t-1} + t^{-1}(z_{t-1} z_{t-1}' - R_{t-1}),$$

where R_t is the moment matrix for z_{t-1} using data $i = 1, ..., t$. As Marcet and Sargent (1989) show the RLS estimator is a *stochastic recursive algorithm* (SRA). A general form of a SRA is given by

$$(2.25) \qquad \theta_t = \theta_{t-1} + \gamma_t Q(t, \theta_{t-1}, X_t),$$

where θ_t is a vector of parameter estimates, X_t is a state vector, and γ_t is a deterministic sequence of "gains". $Q(\cdot)$ is a function that describes how the estimate θ_{t-1} has to be adjusted. Referring to (2.23) and (2.24), θ_{t-1} includes ϕ_{t-1} and R_t, X_t includes z_{t-1} and η_t, and γ_t is equal to t^{-1}.[15]

To answer the question whether the parameters converge to the values that would be obtained under RE, one normally has to study the convergence of a SRA, which is relatively demanding. However, a method called stochastic approximation associates an ordinary difference equation (ODE) with the SRA:

$$(2.26) \qquad \frac{d\theta}{d\tau} = h(\theta(\tau)),$$

where τ denotes "notional" or "artificial"' time. In the case X_t follows an exogenous process – as in our specific example – $h(\theta)$ is obtained as

$$(2.27) \qquad h(\theta(\tau)) = \lim_{t \to \infty} EQ(t, \theta, X_t),$$

provided the limit exists. E expresses the expectations of the function $Q(\cdot)$. However, X_t is also allowed to follow a vector autoregression, where parameters depend on θ_{t-1}. Then $h(\theta)$ is given by

$$(2.28) \qquad h(\theta(\tau)) = \lim_{t \to \infty} EQ(t, \theta, \bar{X}_t(\theta)),$$

where $\bar{X}_t$ is the stochastic process for X_t when θ_{t-1} is held at the fixed value $\theta_{t-1} = \theta$.

According to the stochastic approximation results the behavior of the SRA can be approximated by the behavior of the associated ODE for large t. Honkapohja and Evans (2001, Chapter 6) show that possible limit points of the SRA correspond to the locally stable equilibria of the ODE and arrive

---

[15] Assuming $\gamma_t = t^{-1}$ implies a "decreasing-gain" algorithm, i.e $\gamma_t \to 0$ as $t \to \infty$. Alternatively, one can assume a constant gain, i.e $\gamma_t = \gamma$, where $0 < \gamma < 1$. However, the study of constant gain differs considerably from its decreasing counterpart and thus can lead to different results.

at the following theorem:

Theorem 4:

Under suitable assumptions, if $\bar{\theta}$ is a locally stable equilibrium point of the ODE then $\bar{\theta}$ is a possible point of convergence of the SRA. If $\bar{\theta}$ is not a locally stable equilibrium point of the ODE then $\bar{\theta}$ is not a possible point of convergence of the SRA, i.e. $\theta_t \to \bar{\theta}$ with probability 0.

Moreover, they show that in the case of a unique solution (see theorem 1) and that under the SRA the ODE is globally stable, $\theta_t \to \bar{\theta}$ with probability $1.^{16}$ However, in the case of multiple equilibria (see theorem 3) such a strong result cannot be obtained. We now return to our specific example. Because the REE (2.17) is unique, a globally stable ODE implies convergence.

Defining $R_t = S_{t-1}$ and $E z_t z_t' = M$, and using the fact that $E z_{t-1} \eta_t = 0$ and $\lim_{t \to \infty} t/(t-1) = 1$, the RLS (2.23) and (2.24) can be associated with the following ODE:

$$(2.29) \qquad \frac{d\phi}{d\tau} = h_\phi(\phi) = \lim_{t \to \infty} E\left[S^{-1} z_{t-1} z_{t-1}'(T(\phi) - \phi)\right] = S^{-1}(T(\phi) - \phi),$$

$$(2.30) \qquad \frac{dS}{d\tau} = h_S(S) = \lim_{t \to \infty} E\frac{t}{t-1}(z_t z_t' - S) = M - S.$$

Under the assumption that S is invertible,[17] and because $\lim_{\tau \to \infty} S = M$ from any starting point, and $S^{-1}M = I$ from any starting point, (2.23) and (2.24) we arrive at the smaller dimension system

$$(2.31) \qquad\qquad\qquad \frac{d\phi}{d\tau} = T(\phi) - \phi.$$

If this differential equation is globally stable, $\phi_t \to \bar{\phi}$ as $t \to \infty$. To obtain the ODE (2.31) we used the stochastic approximation tool for SRA. This condition is identical to the so called *E-stability* condition, which was first introduced by Evans (1989) and Evans and Honkapohja (1992). For a wide range of models, the E-stability condition can be obtained by first

---

[16]   Under certain conditions local stability is still sufficient to obtain convergence with probability 1. For a detailed discussion see Chapter 6 in Honkapohja and Evans (2001).

[17]   For technical details see Chapter 6 in Honkapohja and Evans (2001).

defining a mapping from the PLM to the ALM (as for example done in (2.21)). This mapping is then used to establish the E-stability condition given by (2.31). The REE is E-stable if the REE is locally asymptotically stable under equation (2.31), i.e after small deviations from the REE there is a tendency to return to the REE.

In contrast to the quite demanding and tedious analysis of convergence of least squares learning, the E-stability condition is relatively easy to work out and holds for a very wide range of models. Thus, it plays a central role for the study of stability of the REE under adaptive learning.

Before we proceed it will turn out to be useful to give the conditions under which the equilibrium of an ODE such as (2.31) will be stable. In particular, we focus on linear systems of difference equations. Consider a linear system given by

$$(2.32) \qquad \frac{dY}{dt} = AY + B,$$

where Y is a vector of dimension n, A is a n x n coefficient matrix, and B is a matrix of constants that needs not to be specified for what follows. From Sydsaeter et al. (2005) the we obtain the following theorem

Theorem 5:

Suppose that $|A \neq 0|$, then $\frac{dY}{dt} = AY + B$ is globally asymptotically stable if and only if all eigenvalues of A have negative real parts. In the case that one or more eigenvalues have a positive real part, the equilibrium is unstable.

Note that for the special case of $n = 2$, $\frac{dY}{dt} = AY + B$ is globally asymptotically stable if and only if the trace of A is negative and the determinant of A is positive. Otherwise the equilibrium is unstable.

We now set up the E-stability condition for our specific example given by the model (2.16) and a PLM given by (2.18). Using the mapping defined in (2.21) the differential equation which defines E-stability is given by

$$(2.33) \qquad T(\phi) - \phi = \begin{pmatrix} \mu + \alpha a \\ \delta + \alpha b \end{pmatrix} - \begin{pmatrix} a \\ b \end{pmatrix} = \begin{pmatrix} \mu \\ \delta \end{pmatrix} + (\alpha - 1)I \begin{pmatrix} a \\ b \end{pmatrix},$$

where I is the identity matrix. Equation (2.33) is a linear differential equation. Referring to the general form given by (2.32) the vector of state variables is $Y = \begin{pmatrix} a & b \end{pmatrix}'$, the coefficient matrix is $A = (\alpha - 1)I$, and $B = \begin{pmatrix} \mu & \delta \end{pmatrix}'$. According to theorem 5 we need both eigenvalues of $(\alpha - 1)I$ to have negative real parts for (2.33) to be globally asymptotically stable. It is easy to see that the eigenvalues of $(\alpha - 1)I$ are both given by $(\alpha - 1)$. Thus $\begin{pmatrix} \bar{a} & \bar{b} \end{pmatrix}'$ is a globally stable equilibrium point of (2.33) if $\alpha < 1$ and unstable if $\alpha > 1$. In other words, the REE is E-stable if $\alpha < 1$.

2.4.2   Deriving the Taylor principle for a forward-looking Taylor rule under adaptive learning

We consider again the forward-looking interest rate rule given by (2.11). In section 2.3.4 we already showed how to obtain the results for a unique REE. We now ask for the conditions to reach the REE if economic agents form expectations according to the adaptive learning approach.[18]

The *minimal state variable* (MSV) solution (McCallum 1983) for the system of difference equations (2.12) for the REE can be obtained by using the method of undetermined coefficients. With $\mathbf{y} = \begin{pmatrix} x_t & \pi_t \end{pmatrix}'$ and $B = [A_1]^{-1}$ the MSV solution for the REE is given by

$$(2.34) \qquad\qquad\qquad \mathbf{y}_t = \bar{c}\mathbf{v}_t,$$

where $\bar{c} = (I - FA)^{-1}B$.

If the PLM is given by

$$(2.35) \qquad\qquad\qquad E_t^* \mathbf{y}_{t+1} = a + cF\mathbf{v}_t.$$

We obtain the following result:[19]

Proposition 2:

Suppose economic agents from expectations according to (2.35), then under an interest rate rule with forward looking expectations (2.11), the necessary and sufficient condition for the MSV solution (2.34) to be E-stable is that

$$(2.36) \qquad\qquad\qquad \kappa(\phi_x - 1) + (1 - \beta)\phi_x > 0.$$

---

[18]   This problem was first considered by Bullard and Mitra (2002).
[19]   For a detailed proof see Appendix B.

Figure 2.2 gives an illustration for the region of E-Stability.[20] Note that (2.36) is equivalent to condition (2.15), which is the Taylor principle. Thus proposition 1 and 2 show that under an interest rate rule (2.11) a unique MSV solution always includes E-stability. However, E-stability does not necessarily include determinacy of the REE.

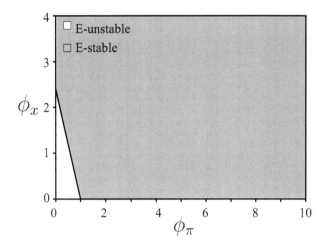

Figure 2.2: E-stability for a forward-looking Taylor rule

Note: Figure 2.2 shows E-stability regions for combinations of ϕ_π and ϕ_x with calibration values of $\beta = 0.99$, $\kappa = 0.024$, $\varphi = \frac{1}{0.157}$ according to Woodford (1999).

2.5 Conclusion

In this chapter we gave a comprehensive treatment for the derivation of the stability conditions for a forward-looking Taylor rule in the basic New Keynesian model under rational expectations and adaptive learning first shown by Bullard and Mitra (2002). To do so, we introduced the basic New Keynesian model according to Gali (2008) and discussed stability conditions. We demonstrated that both under rational expectations and adaptive learning the Taylor principle – the nominal interest rate should be adjusted by more

---

[20]   We use again Woodford's (1999) calibration.

than one-for-one with changes in the inflation rate – plays an important role for stability. However, the Taylor principle gives only a rough guide of how to adjust the interest rate. The response to changes in the output gap is also of importance. For example, if the central bank also puts some weight on the output gap, a stable equilibrium can still be obtained although the Taylor principle does not hold. Moreover, under rational expectation indeterminacy occurs, if the response to the output gap is too aggressive.

Finally, we showed that the critical values of how the nominal interest rate has to be adjusted to changes in the inflation rate and the output gap for a stable equilibrium heavily depend on the specific calibration. For example, whereas Woodford's (1999) calibration would already rule out an output gap coefficient of higher than about 0.3 for determinacy, Clarida's et al. (2000) calibration would still allow for an output gap coefficient of up to 2. Although this observation does not alter the results qualitatively and thus do not seem to be of great importance for economic theory, it can be highly relevant when it comes to the evaluation of empirical studies.

Chapter 3

Inflation targeting makes the difference: Novel evidence on inflation stabilization

3.1   Introduction

In the past decades inflation rates across the globe have been reduced significantly. In the 1980s Latin-American countries experienced the highest inflation rates of all countries averaging more than 200 percent per year. In contrast, in 2007 they had an average inflation rate of about 6 percent. A similar process of declining inflation rates took place in many central and eastern European countries during the 1990s. As a group, these countries reduced their inflation rates substantially from, on average, 45 percent per year in the 1990s down to, on average, 5 percent per year in 2007. This process of stabilizing inflation was achieved under fairly different monetary and exchange rate regimes, ranging from the adoption of inflation targeting combined with floating exchange rates to the abandonment of independent monetary policy by introducing currency boards or even by dollarization of the economy.

While all stabilization strategies aim to increase central bank credibility in order to stabilize inflation expectations and, thus, inflation itself, inflation targeting is the most prominent strategy and, hence, has gained substantial support among the economics profession. So has the use of Taylor rules for characterizing central banks' behavior. Even though theoretically inflation targeting is proven to be consistent with monetary policy rules (Svensson, 1997, 2003), empirical evidence in favor of the effectiveness of inflation targeting has not yet provided. On the one hand, studies find support that inflation rates have decreased in inflation targeting countries (Corbo et al., 2002; Landerrechte et al., 2001), however, it is less clear whether this is due to the introduction of inflation targeting since this effect also occurs in non-inflation targeting countries (Mishkin and Schmidt-Hebbel, 2006). On the other hand, literature so far fails to show that central banks indeed act stabilizing once inflation targeting is introduced (Mehrotra and Sánchez-Fung, 2009; Brito and Bysted, 2010). This chapter aims to close this research gap.

We provide strong and unique evidence that the introduction of inflation targeting has changed the behavior of monetary policy authorities in the sense that once a country introduces inflation targeting, the inflation coefficient in its monetary policy rule increases significantly to values above unity for the majority of inflation targeting countries. This feature reflects the Taylor principle and it is strongly associated with economic stability (Gali, 2008). We also shed light on the aspect whether central banks in inflation targeting countries have actually done what they praise. Since we show that central banks' officially announced inflation target is consistent with the long-term inflation rate based on the central bank's behavior, we conclude that many inflation targeting central banks, indeed, follow their official announcements of inflation targets.

To this end, we use a data set which allows us to exactly estimate the effect of inflation targeting for a large number of countries. This identification strategy is superior to comparing inflation targeting to non-inflation targeting countries since this method neglect country specific characteristics (Mishkin and Schmidt-Hebbel, 2006). Our data set and research strategy is similar to Crowe (2010) and allows us to directly measure the impact of an inflation targeting regime. Crowe (2010) shows that the adoption of inflation targeting promotes the convergence in forecast errors for eleven countries suggesting that the adoption enhances transparency. Our data set is unique since it is available to the central banks in real-time, frequently published and reflects the forward-looking nature of central bank's policy. Furthermore, it allows us to compare the results among a large number of countries since the characteristics of the data are the same among all countries. All this together is essential to describe a central banks reaction function in reality.

This chapter continues as follows. The subsequent Section 2 briefly reviews the commonly applied empirical concept of Taylor-type rules. Section 3.3 introduces the data set. Sections 3.4 and 3.5 present the empirical results.

Section 3.6 studies the importance of the time-varying inflation target and time-varying inflation coefficients. Finally, Section 3.7 concludes.

3.2 The empirical morphology of Taylor-type rules

All major central banks in industrial and emerging economies currently conduct monetary policy by using market-oriented instruments in order to influence the short-term interest rate. Since the seminal paper of Taylor (1993), it has virtually become a convention to describe the interest rate setting behavior of central banks in terms of monetary policy reaction functions.[1] In its plain form, the so-called Taylor rule states that the short-term interest rate, i.e., the instrument of a central bank, reacts to deviations of inflation and output from their respective target levels. Although the Taylor rule started out as an empirical exercise, there is a clear theoretical link between optimal (inflation targeting) monetary policy and Taylor rules. Among others, Svensson (1997, 2003) showed that (contemporaneous and forward-looking) Taylor rules can be derived as the explicit solution of an optimal control problem within stylized macro models.

For the purpose of empirical exercises in a seminal paper Clarida et al. (1998) propose a specific forward-looking variant of the Taylor rule which takes into account the pre-emptive nature of monetary policy as well as interest smoothing behavior of central banks. This particular type of reaction function has become very popular in applied empirical research. Although it is still in the spirit of the Taylor rule, specifications of this type represent a modification of the original Taylor rule and, thus, the literature often refers to them as Taylor-type rules. Following Clarida et al. (1998, 2000) and Taylor (1999) the baseline forward-looking policy rule takes the form:

$$(3.1) \qquad i_t^* = \bar{i} + \alpha_1 E_t(\pi_{t+k} - \pi^*) + \alpha_2 E_t(y_{t+k} - y_{t+k}^*),$$

where i^* is the desired level of the nominal short-term interest rate, and $\bar{i}$ is its equilibrium level. The second term on the right-hand side is the expected deviation of the k-period ahead inflation rate (π) from the target rate (π^*)

---

[1] Note that this section heavliy borrows from Rülke (2009), who estimated Ex-ante Taylor-type rules for the G7.

which is assumed to be constant over time.[2] The third term is the expected deviation of the k-period ahead level of output (y) from its natural level (y^*), i.e., the expected output gap $E(\hat{y}_t)$. The coefficients α_1 and α_2 which will be the center of our estimates represent the reaction coefficients.

The coefficient for the inflation gap α_1 is of particular importance. In order to act in a stabilizing manner it has to be greater than unity, which is referred to as the well-known *Taylor principle*. The central bank has to react with its nominal policy rate more than proportional than the underlying inflation shocks in order to increase to real interest rate. If the *Taylor principle* does not hold, the central bank reaction leads to a declining real interest rate in the case of rising inflation which clearly is at odds with stabilization efforts.

The additional assumption of interest rate smoothing behavior implies that:

$$(3.2) \qquad\qquad i_t = (1 - \rho)i_t^* + \rho i_{t-1} + \nu_t,$$

with the parameter ρ representing the degree of interest rate smoothing (with $0 < \rho < 1$) and ν_t represents an i.i.d. exogenous random shock to the interest rate. Combining Equations (3.1) and (3.2) leads to

$$(3.3) \quad i_t = (1 - \rho)(\bar{i} + \alpha_1 E_t(\pi_{t+k} - \pi^*) + \alpha_2 E_t(y_{t+k} - y_{t+k}^*)) + \rho i_{t-1} + \nu_t.$$

Equation (3.3) represents the econometric specification which is commonly used to describe central bank behavior.[3] It is reduced to the plain Taylor rule when ρ is zero and the horizon of the forward-looking behavior of the central bank, k, is also set equal to zero in econometric exercises.

The main messages generated by empirical studies focusing on central bank behavior in industrial countries can be summarized as follows. First, forward-looking specifications seem to fit the central banks' behavior better

---

[2]   In the subsequent analysis we allow the inflation target π^* to be time variant. This actually fits reality very well against the background that inflation targeting countries frequently announce inflation targets reflecting nothing else than the desired long-term inflation rate. As these countries are trying to decrease the perceived long-term inflation level they are announcing decreasing inflation targets.

[3]   Since it contains expectations on the right-hand side that are not directly observable it is common to substitute them by the observed ex-post levels of the respective variables and rearrange the estimation equation into a form that contains the expectation errors of the central bank in the error term. This form is then estimated based on the General Methods of Moments.

than contemporaneous versions. Here the forward-looking feature is most relevant for the inflation gap with the horizon (k) being about one year. Second, the relevance of the *Taylor principle* for stability is well demonstrated and its presence is a strong feature for most central banks. Third, the reaction coefficient for the output gap is mostly statistically significant but has a lower level compared to the inflation gap coefficient.[4] Fourth, persistence in the short-term interest rate is a strong feature found in the data. However, what is not yet clear is whether this is due to intended interest rate smoothing or whether it is due to a strong autocorrelation in the shocks upon which monetary policy reacts.[5]

Subsequently, we estimate variants of Equation (3.3) based on reported forecasts of financial market participants. We believe that for several reasons to be discussed below private forecasts on inflation and output are suitable for the estimation of forward-looking Taylor rules. Gorter et al. (2008), for example, use private sector forecasts to show that the European Central Bank is Taylor-rule based. Before we present and discuss the empirical results, the next section briefly introduces our data set.

3.3 The data set

We use inflation and GDP growth forecasts published in the survey conducted by Consensus Economics for the time period between January 1990 and December 2007.[6] [7] During this time 23 inflation targeting countries have been surveyed by Consensus Economics. Since we only include inflation targeting countries which have a sufficient number of observations this limits our analysis to 18 countries.[8]

---

[4]   In particular, for the output gap the literature demonstrated that it is relevant to discriminate between ex post and real-time data (Orphanides, 2001). Since we use observed expected variables in our analysis all variables are available to the central bank in real-time.

[5]   Again, since this issue is also not of a strong concern in this chapter, we refer to the recent literature. See, for instance, Rudebusch (2006).

[6]   We choose to end our sample period in 2007 to separate the impact of inflation targeting from the influence of the economic and financial crisis 2008-2009.

[7]   Note that for the description of the data set we heavily borrow from Rülke (2009), who used Consensus Economics data to estimate the expectation formation process in inflation targeting emerging markets economies.

[8]   Since we do not have observations for the inflation targeting period for Australia, Indonesia, Serbia, South Korea and Thailand, we skip these countries.

There are several reasons of why the data set of the Consensus Economic poll should be of interest for the central bank and hence, is suitable to estimate a forward-looking monetary policy rule.[9] First, the survey participants work with the private sector in the respective country[10] and hence, should report a true notion of the expected economic development. The fact that we use private sector forecasts is also of advantage compared to the forecasts of international institutions or even the central bank itself. While the latter might have an incentive to report strategic forecasts consistent with their macroeconomic policy, the private sector should have an incentive to provide an accurate forecast rather than a strategic forecast. Batchelor (2001) shows that the Consensus Economics forecasts are less biased and more accurate in terms of mean absolute error and root mean square error compared to OECD and IMF forecasts. Moreover, the individual forecasts are published along the names of the forecaster and its affiliation. Since analysts are bound in their survey answers by their recommendations to clients an analyst may find it hard to justify why he gave a recommendation different to the one in the survey. Given that this allows everybody to evaluate the performance of the individual participants, the accuracy of the forecasts can be expected to have an effect on the reputation of the forecasters.[11]

Second, since the poll is conducted each month during the first week and released within the second week, it is a *timely* and *frequent* disseminational means for the central bank to get to know how inflation and growth expectation develop. Since in most developing and emerging market economies actual inflation and growth rates are reported by the federal statistical office only on a quarterly basis, if at all and with a substantial period of time lag, this data set provides central banks with relevant and recent information of macroeconomic trends. Third, the forecasts are not revised and, hence not exposed to the *real-time data critique.* Orphanides (2001) shows that it is crucial to distinguish between real-time and revised data to correctly assess the information set on which the central bank sets its interest rate decisions.

---

[9]   Gorter et al. (2008) use the Consensus Economics poll to estimate a Taylor-type rule for the ECB. Compared to this, Bernanke and Woodford (1997) show that strict inflation targeting based on private sector forecasts is inconsistent with the existence of rational expectations equilibrium, and that policies approximating strict inflation-forecast targeting are likely to have undesirable properties.

[10]   The participants are professional economists working for universities and financial institutions such as international economic research institutes, investment and commercial banks. Further information concerning the survey can be found in the website: www.consensuseconomics.com.

[11]   Dovern und Weisser (2008) show that forecasters in the Consensus Economic survey provide rational forecasts.

This issue is most likely to be even more important for emerging countries which report the inflation rate and growth rate with a substantial time lag, revise them frequently or do not officially publish any information that can be used to estimate a central bank reaction function. Fourth, the data set allows us to compare the results among the countries since each forecasted variable is the same among in all surveys. Hence, our analysis does not suffer from problems arising in different reporting standards.

Consensus Economics publishes the forecasts for two different time horizons, namely the current and the next year. We weighted both forecasts with the remaining months at the time of the forecast to obtain a fixed forecast horizon of twelve months.[12] The length of the forecast horizon of twelve months can be justified by the time-lag of the monetary policy transmission which is about twelve months (Friedman, 1961). Applying different forecast horizons does not change our results qualitatively. This procedure is quite common in the literature (Gorter et al. 2008, Heppke-Falk and Hüffner, 2004, and Beck, 2001).

Table 3.1 provides an overview of the characteristics of the data set for the 18 inflation targeting countries for the period before and after the introduction of inflation targeting. Table 3.1 also reports the sample period and the date of the introduction of inflation targeting.[13] Interestingly, our sample period covers the period previous and after the introduction of inflation targeting for all countries but New Zealand for which we only have data for the inflation targeting period.[14] In contrast to other studies who compare inflation targeting to non-inflation targeting countries (Mishkin and Schmidt-Hebbel, 2006), this unique data set allows us to exactly identify the impact of the introduction of inflation targeting. Table 3.1 also shows that, in principle, the forecasts coincides with the actual series for the majority of countries. This applies for the period before and after the introduction of inflation targeting. For instance, for Colombia the expected inflation rate

---

[12] See Appendix C for a detailed formula for the calculation of the weighted expectations.

[13] Mishkin and Schmidt-Hebbel (2006) provide an excellent overview of inflation targeting countries.

[14] We define a country to be an inflation targeting country exclusively for time periods when inflation targeting has been the central bank's *official* monetary policy regime. This *de jure* approach is consistent with Roger (2009). Note that several central banks, including the European Central Bank, the Swiss National Bank, and the Federal Reserve Bank, have many attributes of inflation targeting. However, they do not *officially* adopt inflation targeting as a monetary policy strategy. Moreover, an increasing number of such attributes oftentimes can be observed in time periods just before a country officially adopts inflation targeting.

before (after) the introduction of inflation targeting is about 19 (6) percent while the actual value is about 20 (7) percent. In our analysis the interest rate is either the money market rate or an appropriate alternative short-term interest rate. The choice of the interest rate was based on data availability.[15]

As a showcase Figures 3.1, 3.2, and 3.3 display the inflation target[16], the interest rate, the expected and actual inflation rate for Brazil, Mexico, Poland and South Africa. Though the actual inflation rate and expected inflation move in line, inflation expectations are less volatile. The figures provide anecdotical evidence that the central banks respond to inflation expectations rather than the actual inflation rate. For instance, for Brazil during the Latin-American crisis in 1999 the inflation expectations increased substantially from 3 percent up to 15 percent while the actual inflation rate remained relatively low at five percent. During this time the central bank of Brazil increased its interest rate from 20 to 40 percent and hence seemed to respond to private inflation expectations rather than the actual inflation rate. In Mexico between 1999 and 2001 the inflation rate increased up to 50 percent while private inflation expectations remained low at about 10 percent. During that period the central bank of Mexico decreased its interest rate and hence reacted to the relatively low inflation expectations rather then to the temporary inflationary shock. The same picture arises in South Africa between 2001 and 2003 (Figure 3.3) where the inflation rate picked up from 3 to 13 percent while inflation expectations remained at 6 percent and the interest rate did not change noticeably.

---

[15]   For Brazil, Czech Republic, Finland, New Zealand, Spain and Turkey we used the money market rate from the IMF; for Hungary, Israel and Romania we used the deposit rate from the IMF; for Chily we used the central bank's monetary policy rate; for Columbia we used the central bank's interbank overnight rate; for Mexico we used the central bank's monetary policy rate; for Norway we used the next day interbank rate; for Peru we used saving rate; for Poland we used the one week interbank rate; for South Africa we we used a three month T-Bill rate; for Sweden we used the one week interbank rate.

[16]   We use historical inflation targets publicly announced by the central banks. To obtain these historical inflation targets we consulted inflation reports or other publications of the central banks. Sometimes central banks announce a target range. In such cases we take the mean of the target range. This procedure will turn out to be useful for our econometric analysis below.

Table 3.1: Overview of the inflation targeting countries (1990 - 2007)

Country (IT Since) Period	Inflation Forecast Pre-IT	IT	Actual Inflation Rate Pre-IT	IT	Nominal Interest Rate Pre-IT	IT	Real Interest Rate Pre-IT	IT
Brazil (Jun 99) Jan 95 - Dec 07	11.23	5.88	39.69	7.24	33.97	14.67	22.74	8.79
Chile§ (Sep 99) Mar 93 - Dec 07	5.28	4.70	7.51	3.06	13.80	4.90	8.52	0.20
Columbia (Sep 99) Mar 93 - Dec 07	18.87	6.03	19.69	6.55	25.11	6.31	6.24	0.28
Czech Rep. (Dec 97) Dec 94 - Dec 07	8.47	4.09	8.91	3.41	12.85	4.85	4.38	0.76
Finland† (Jan 93) Jan 90 - Dec 98	8.47	2.30	4.28	1.23	13.44	4.88	4.97	2.58
Hungary (Jun 01) Nov 90 - Dec 07	4.85	5.08	20.70	5.61	19.61	7.65	14.76	2.57
Israel (Jan 97) Dec 94 - Dec 07	9.9	3.35	10.85	2.90	14.38	7.05	4.48	3.70
Mexico (Jan 01) Jan 90 - Dec 07	16.05	4.14	21.60	11.55	24.32	7.82	8.27	3.68
New Zealand‡ (Jan 90) Jan 90 - Dec 94	–	3.04	–	2.56	–	8.15	–	5.11
Norway (Mar 01) Jan 90 - Dec 07	2.94	1.85	2.52	1.65	8.09	3.45	5.15	1.60
Peru (Jan 02) Mar 93 - Dec 07	11.64	2.28	12.65	1.92	10.67	3.04	-0.97	0.76
Poland (Oct 98) Nov 90 - Dec 07	32.73	4.00	122.57	4.00	28.27	6.81	-4.46	2.81
Romania (Aug 05) Dec 94 - Dec 07	35.53	5.77	44.62	6.21	31.06	5.55	-4.47	-0.22
Slovakia (Jan 05) Dec 94 - Dec 07	8.01	2.96	7.84	3.32	10.78	3.59	2.77	0.63
South Africa (Feb 02) Jun 93 - Dec 07	8.47	5.11	7.24	4.23	14.51	9.13	6.04	4.02
Spain† (Jan 95) Jan 90 - Dec 98	5.38	3.12	5.58	3.01	11.78	6.17	6.40	3.05
Sweden (Jan 93) Jan 90 - Dec 07	6.31	1.96	7.41	1.50	13.70	4.57	7.39	2.61
Turkey (Jan 06) Dec 94 - Dec 07	57.49	7.53	56.11	9.65	55.71	16.41	-1.78	8.88

Notes: All reported values are averages based on monthly data except for New Zealand's actual inflation rate which is based on quarterly data; The inflation targets are obtained from the monthly inflation reports; If a country announces an inflation target band, we used the average of the inflation target band as proposed by Mishkin and Schmidt-Hebbel (2006); † Due to the introduction of the Euro, the series ends in December 1998. ‡ The series already ends in December 1994 due to data availability; § On July 26, 2001 the Board of the Banco Central de Chile decided, as from August 9, 2001, to define the monetary policy rate in nominal terms, i.e. as a percentage in relation to a value in pesos and not in *Unidad de Formento* (UF) as before. Since then the nominal annual interest rate was set at 6.5%, which corresponded to the monetary policy rate of UF plus 3.5%. This number is derived from the target of the real interest of 3.5% and the mean of the range of the inflation target. Thus, to compare the monetary policy rate before and after August 2001, we add the inflation target to the monetary policy rate before August 2001.

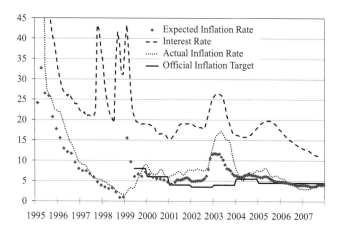

Figure 3.1: Inflation target, interest rate, expected and actual inflation rate in Brazil

Note: Figure 3.1 shows the inflation target (solid line), interest rate (dotted line), actual inflation rate (fine dotted line) and the twelve-month ahead expected inflation rate (squares) at time t.

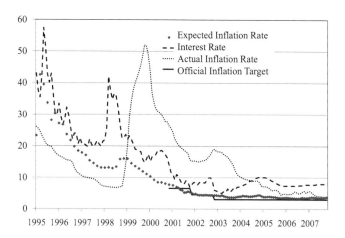

Figure 3.2: Inflation target, interest rate, expected and actual inflation rate in Mexico

Note: Figure 3.2 shows the inflation target (solid line), interest rate (dotted line), actual inflation rate (fine dotted line) and the twelve-month ahead expected inflation rate (squares) at time t.

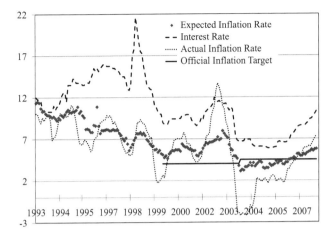

Figure 3.3: Inflation target, interest rate, expected and actual inflation rate in South Africa

Note: Figure 3.3 shows the inflation target (solid line), interest rate (dotted line), actual inflation rate (fine dotted line) and the twelve-month ahead expected inflation rate (squares) at time t.

3.4 Estimation results

Our empirical analysis starts from the econometric specification of the Taylor-type rule as presented in Equation (3.3). The most difficult variable to quantify in this framework is the expected output gap. Due to the before-mentioned data availability, we use the output growth forecasts rather than for the output gap. For this reason, we slightly depart from specification (3.3) and estimate the following specification:

$$(3.4) \qquad i_t = (1 - \rho)(\bar{i} + \alpha_1 E_t(\pi_{t+k} - \pi^*) + \alpha_2 E_t \Delta y_{t+k}) + \rho i_{t-1} + \nu_t,$$

where the output gap has been substituted by the growth rate of output. The inclusion of such an output growth term has been shown to offer a simple characterization of historical monetary policy in several studies (Orphanides, 2003; McCallum and Nelson, 1999; Levin et al., 1999, 2003).

Since most inflation targeting countries are small open economies, interest rate decisions might be based on the exchange rate development. Stone et al. (2009) argue that the real exchange rate plays an important role in monetary policy for emerging market economies that have adopted inflation targeting. However, they note that under a specification such as Equation (3.4) where the exchange rate does not enter explicitly, the exchange rate developments and prospects are taken into account implicitly because they affect the inflation and output forecast. In addition, Taylor (2001, p. 267), notes that "[...] monetary policy rules that react directly to the exchange rate as well as to inflation and output, do not work much better in stabilizing inflation and real output and sometimes work worse than policy rules that do not react directly to the exchange rate". Ball (1998), Svensson (2000), and Bharucha and Kent (1998) show that inflation targeting central banks pay too much attention to exchange rate fluctuations.

Since the focus of our study exclusively lies on the question of inflation stabilizing, we do not include a real exchange rate into the central bank reaction function directly. This can be justified since almost all emerging economies that are included in our data set are classified as *full-fledged inflation targeting emerging economies* for the inflation targeting period. That is, they have a floating exchange rate (independent or managed float), and they make a clear commitment to an inflation target (Stone et al., 2009). Only Hungary and the Slovak Republic had an exchange rate peg of ± 15 percent to the Euro under the ERM II regime whilst they operated in an inflation targeting framework.

In order to arrive at a testable relationship, the unobservable terms in Equation (3.4) have to be eliminated. Since our data set allows us to directly observe the interest rate, the expected inflation rate and the expected growth rate, we only lack information on the equilibrium interest rate and the inflation target. Consistent with Clarida et al. (1998), we treat these two variables as time-invariant and aggregate both of them into the constant.[17] Thus, we rewrite Equation (3.4) as:

$$(3.5) \quad i_t = (1-\rho)\alpha_0 + \alpha_1(1-\rho)E_t\pi_{t+k} + \alpha_2(1-\rho)E_t\Delta y_{t+k} + \rho i_{t-1} + \nu_t,$$

where

$$(3.6) \qquad\qquad\qquad \alpha_0 = \bar{i} - \alpha_1 E\pi^*.$$

In order to analyze whether the introduction of inflation targeting has changed the monetary policy behavior towards (more) inflation stabilization, we define a dummy (D_{IT}) which is equal to one in the inflation targeting regime and zero otherwise. In order to examine whether the introduction has changed the monetary policy response to inflation, we interact the dummy

---

[17]   In Section 3.6 we allow for an observable time-varying inflation target.

with the coefficient λ. This allows us to test whether the monetary policy rule has changed after the introduction of inflation targeting. Thus, we rewrite Equation (3.5) as:

$$i_t = (1 - \rho)\alpha_0 + \alpha_1(1 - \rho)E_t\pi_{t+k} + \lambda(1 - \rho)E_t\pi_{t+k} \cdot D_{IT}$$
(3.7)
$$+ \alpha_2(1 - \rho)E_t\Delta y_{t+k} + \rho i_{t-1} + \nu_t.$$

The coefficient of the interaction term (λ) reflects the difference in the inflation coefficient before and after the introduction of inflation targeting. From its size and significance together with the estimates of the pre-inflation targeting coefficient (α_1) we can infer the size and the significance of the coefficient (α_1^{IT}) which measured the response to inflation expectations during the inflation targeting period.

The first column of Table 3.2 reports the results of Equation (3.7) for all inflation targeting countries in a panel fixed-effects model.[18] The inflation coefficient of the pre-inflation targeting period (α_1) is significantly positive and about .25. This reflects that the countries on average increase its interest rate by .25 percent if the expected inflation rate increases by one percent. Hence, the real interest rate decreases by approximately .75 percent. This implies that the *Taylor principle is violated* for the time period before the introduction of inflation targeting. Compared to that, the *Taylor principle holds* for the period after the introduction since the inflation coefficient α_1^{IT} of about 1.67 is significantly higher than unity.

Although all variables on the right-hand side are also observed data and thus are exogenously, as a robustness test, we treat the forecasts as endogenous variables end estimate Equation (3.7) based on the generalized methods of moments (GMM). As instruments for the inflation and output forecasts we use the contemporaneous actual inflation rate as well as its first to twelfth lag, the first and second lag of the inflation rate forecast and of the inflation forecast dummy, the first lag of output growth forecast and the contemporaneous real effective exchange as well as its first, second and third lag. Table 3.2 (second column) reports the results based on the GMM fixed-effect panel estimator[19] which are similar to the fixed effects estimates.

---

[18] Since stationarity is a prerequisite to estimate Taylor rules to avoid the spurious regression problem (Österholm, 2005), we tested for stationarity in our data which cannot be rejected on a one percent level.

[19] Note that we do not report a constant here, since we use a *two-step feasible GMM* estimation with minimum asymptotic variance that are heteroscedasticity- and autocorrelation-consistent (Baum et al., 2007).

The inflation coefficient of the pre-inflation targeting period (α_1) is again significantly positive and of about .65. which violates the *Taylor principle*. Compared to this, the *Taylor principle* holds for the inflation targeting period since the inflation coefficient (α_1^{IT}) is 1.44 and significantly higher than unity.

As a diagnostic check and robustness tests, Table 3.2 reports the p-values of several test statistics. The p-value of the Hansen J-static of .24 suggests that the instruments are uncorrelated with the error term, since the null cannot be rejected at a ten percent level. The F-test rejects the null hypothesis of weakly correlated instruments and the Kleibergen-Paap test as well as the Angrist-Pischke test show that our model is identified. The fact that the fixed-effects model and the GMM estimate yield qualitatively similar results supports Gorter et al. (2008) who estimate a Taylor-type rule for the ECB and conclude that endogeneity is not a concern when using the Consensus Economics data.

The results reported in Table 3.2 also show that the central banks have a substantial degree of interest rate smoothing of about .86 and do not systematically respond to changes in the expected growth rate. It is tempting to interpret this result as evidence that the countries follow a strict inflation targeting regime. However, it could also be the case that the output measure does not reflect the central banks target of the real economic. Since we slightly depart from the standard Taylor-type rule we assume that the central bank responds to high growth rates with an increase in the interest rate. However, if actual output is still lower than potential output the central bank might not be tempted to increase the interest rate. Therefore, the expected GDP growth variable does not perfectly reflect the monetary policy response to the real economic.

Since our panel analysis so far assumes that all central banks respond to the same extent to expected inflation, i.e. all have the same inflation coefficient, we subsequently estimate Equation (3.7) for each country individually. Table 3.3 reports the results for each country based on a Newey-West estimator to account for serial correlation in the error term (Newey and West, 1987).[20] The column 'α_1' reflecting the inflation coefficient for the pre-inflation targeting period shows that the *Taylor principle*, i.e. $\alpha_1 > 1$, only holds for six countries, namely Brazil, Colombia, the Czech Republic, Israel, Norway and Spain. The column 'α_1^{IT}' reporting the inflation coefficient for the inflation targeting period shows that for twelve countries α_1^{IT} is

---

[20]   As a robustness test we also used other estimation techniques, such as the seemingly unrelated regressor to account for cross section correlation.

Table 3.2: Panel Taylor-type rule

Estimator	Time-Constant		Time-Varying	
	Fixed-Effect	GMM	Fixed-Effect	GMM
α_0	14.46*	-	5.62*	-
	(1.14)		(.37)	
α_1	.25*	.65*	-	-
	(.04)	(.11)		
α_1^{IT}	1.67*	1.44*	1.83*	2.07*
	(.25)	(.19)	(.16)	(.36)
α_2	-.44	-.06	-.05	-.05
	(.24)	(.21)	(.09)	(.09)
ρ	.86*	.86*	.92*	.93*
	(.01)	(.04)	(.01)	(.01)
$\alpha_1^{IT} > \alpha_1$	.00	.00	-	-
$\alpha_1 > 1$	.99	.99	-	-
$\alpha_1^{IT} > 1$	.00	.00	.00	.00
Hausman	.00	-	.00	-
R^2	.94	.91	.99	.97
Obs.	2,406	2,147	1,313	1,238
Wald-test	-	.00	-	.00
Hansen J statistic	-	.24	-	.16
K.-P.rk LM statistics	-	.00	-	.00
A.-P. Chi-squared α_1; α_1^{IT}; α_2	-	.00; .00; .00	-	-; .00; .00

Notes: Estimated equation (3.7) $i_t = (1 - \rho)\alpha_0 + \alpha_1(1 - \rho)E_t\pi_{t+k} + \lambda(1 - \rho)E_t\pi_{t+k} \cdot D_{IT} + \alpha_2(1 - \rho)E_t(\Delta y_{t+k}) + \rho i_{t-1} + \nu_t$; values in parentheses represent panel corrected standard errors applying the Prais-Winsten model for the fixed-effects model estimates; GMM estimates are based on *two-step feasible GMM* estimation with minimum asymptotic variance that are heteroscedasticity- and autocorrelation-consistent; as instruments for the forecast variables we use the contemporaneous actual inflation rate as well as its first to twelfth lag, the first and second lag of the inflation rate forecast and the inflation forecast dummy, the first lag of the GDP growth forecast and the contemporaneous real effective exchange as well as its first, second and third lag; the null hypothesis of the Wald-test is whether the instruments are weakly correlated with endogenous regressors; the Kleinbergen-Paap (K.-P.) rank LM test and the Angrist-Pischke (A.-P.) first-stage chi-squared test are underidentification tests of whether the model is identified meaning the instruments are relevant where the null hypothesis states that the model is not identified; the Hansen J statistic tests the null hypothesis whether the instruments are uncorrelated with the error terms; for all tests we present p-values; the Hausman test suggests to use the fixed-effects estimator on a one percent significance level; $\alpha_1 > 1$ and $\alpha_1^{IT} > 1$ represents the significance level of a Chi^2 test to test whether the *Taylor-principle* holds with the null hypothesis that $\alpha_1 \leq 1$ and $\alpha_1^{IT} \leq 1$; $\alpha_1^{IT} > \alpha_1 > 1$ represents the significance level of a Chi^2 test to test whether the pre-inflation coefficient and the inflation coefficient are different with the null hypothesis that $\alpha_1^{IT} \leq \alpha_1$; R^2 refers to the overall coefficient of determination; for readability within and between R^2 are left from the Table but available upon request; * indicates significance at the one percent level, respectively.

significantly larger than unity while only Hungary has an inflation coefficient smaller than unity.[21]

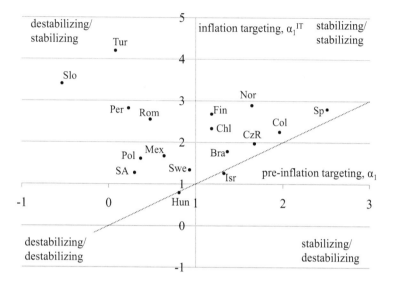

Figure 3.4: Inflation coefficient for the (pre-)inflation targeting period

Note: Figure 3.4 shows the inflation coefficient for the (pre-)inflation targeting period on the vertical (horizontal) axis. Countries in the upper right (lower left) show (de-)stabilizing monetary policy in both periods while countries in the upper left are countries which have (de-)stabilizing monetary policy in the (pre-)inflation targeting period. The dotted line reflects a 45 degree line and indicates whether the introduction of inflation targeting has affected monetary policy stabilization.

For Chile, Finland, Mexico, New Zealand, Peru, Slovakia and Turkey, the inflation coefficient is larger than unity for the inflation targeting pe-

---

[21] Note that between 2001 and 2004 Hungary targeted the exchange rate within a ±15 percent band whilst it operated in an inflation targeting framework. Stone et al. (2009) argue that speculative attacks and deterioration of market confidence caused conflicts between both targets in 2003. As a consequence, after 2004 the Magyar Nemzeti Bank (MNB) did no longer announce a preferred exchange rate. In February 2008, the exchange rate band was abandoned and price stability became the primary objective of the MNB. The turmoil in 2003 thus might be seen as an explanation for Hungary's poor performance regarding inflation stabilizing. More generally, the case of Hungary points out potential problems that can arise if an inflation targeting central bank also tries to follow an exchange rate target.

riod only. This indicates that for these countries the introduction of inflation targeting has a direct impact of the central banks response to inflation expectations. For eleven countries, we find that α_1^{IT} is significantly higher α_1 reflecting that the response to inflation expectations increased for the majority of countries once inflation targeting is introduced. This implies that the central bank reaction is consistent with the central bank's communication towards fighting inflationary pressure in inflation targeting periods.

To provide a graphical illustration of the impact of the introduction of inflation targeting on the central bank reaction function, Figure 3.4 shows the inflation coefficient for the (pre-)inflation targeting period on the (horizontal) vertical axis. All countries but Hungary and Israel are above the 45 degree line and, hence, respond stronger to inflation expectations in the inflation targeting period. Moreover, the figure shows that eight countries are located in the upper left and, hence, shifted their monetary policy towards inflation stabilizing once they have introduced inflation targeting. Compared to this, the eight countries in the upper right have ever stabilized inflation. Only, Hungary located in the lower left has not stabilized inflation for both periods.

Table 3.3 also shows that only Colombia, New Zealand and Spain increase the interest rate if the expected growth increases. This result does not change if one differentiates between before and after the introduction of inflation targeting. The constant term is significant for most countries. Since the constant term captures the long-term inflation rate (π^*) one can analyze the long-term target of the central banks by means of the results obtained in Table 3.3.

3.5 Expectations on the long-term inflation rate

The estimation procedure enables us to investigate another feature inherent in the Taylor-type rule. Equation (3.7) allows us to calculate the long-term inflation rate (π^*) on which the monetary policy is based. In order to recover the long-term inflation rate (π^*) we can use the parameter estimates α_0 and α_1 (α_1^{IT}) from Table 3.3. Recall that

$$(3.8) \qquad \alpha_0 = \bar{i} - \alpha_1 E\pi^*$$

and given the Fisher relation

$$(3.9) \qquad \bar{i} = r + E\pi^*$$

Chapter 3. Inflation targeting

Table 3.3: Individual Taylor-type rules

Count.	α_0	α_1	α_1^{IT}	α_2	ρ	$\alpha_1^{IT} > \alpha_1$	$\alpha_1 > 1$	$\alpha_1^{IT} > 1$	R^2	Obs.
	20.09*	1.36*	1.78*	-2.66+	.80*	.22	.01	.02	.97	118
Bra	(3.58)	(.15)	(.40)	(.72)	(.05)					
	4.94*	1.18*	2.33*	-.22	.39*	.00	.30	.00	.78	129
Chl	(2.07)	(.34)	(.33)	(.04)	(.10)					
	-12.02	1.96*	2.25*	2.62+	.77*	.08	.01	.00	.90	117
Col	-7.83	(.39)	(.34)	(1.36)	(.09)					
	.82	1.67*	1.97*	-.44	.71*	.08	.00	.00	.94	103
CzR	(1.40)	(.16)	(.30)	(.37)	(.14)					
	6.03	1.18	2.68*	-.39	.90*	.02	.40	.00	.98	105
Fin	(4.20)	(.72)	(.50)	(.61)	(.04)					
	4.00	.81*	.79*	-.37	.92*	.97	.74	.74	.99	151
Hun	(8.60)	(.29)	(.32)	(1.27)	(.04)					
	2.90+	1.32*	1.26*	-.44	.89*	.76	.01	.16	.99	155
Isr	(1.61)	(.14)	(.26)	(.37)	(.04)					
	6.28	.64+	1.67*	.86	.77*	.04	.96	.05	.95	168
Mex	(6.30)	(.21)	(.41)	(1.62)	(.10)					
	-7.54+	–	2.61*	3.06*	.79*	–	–	.00	.92	59
NZ	(2.86)	–	(.46)	(.83)	(.10)					
	2.76*	1.64*	2.89*	-.04	.68	.00	.01	.00	.98	215
Nor	(1.24)	(.27)	(.32)	(.27)	(.10)					
	6.43*	.23*	2.82*	.41	.85*	.00	.99	.00	.98	129
Per	(2.79)	(.07)	(.40)	(.56)	(.12)					
	10.01	.37	1.61+	.24	.95*	.22	.99	.24	.98	152
Pol	(10.87)	(.26)	(.86)	(1.62)	(.04)					
	16.04	.48	2.55	-.06	.87*	.37	.78	.21	.89	103
Rom	(28.02)	(.69)	(1.91)	(3.70)	(.09)					
	13.22*	-.54	3.41*	.58	.55*	.03	.97	.05	.59	103
Slo	(10.78)	(.83)	(1.43)	(1.22)	(.17)					
	11.03+	.30	1.27*	.38	.95*	.01	.94	.27	.97	175
SA	(4.44)	(.49)	(.44)	(1.20)	(.02)					
	-4.95*	2.51*	2.80*	1.11*	.86*	.07	.00	.00	.99	107
Sp	(1.45)	(.29)	(.32)	(.33)	(.06)					
	7.20+	.93	1.34*	-1.43+	.52*	.51	.56	.19	.66	214
Swe	(3.61)	(.40)	(.39)	(.73)	(.14)					
	77.33*	.08	4.20*	-5.92	.77*	.03	.99	.04	.78	103
Tur	(17.49)	(.17)	(1.76)	(3.62)	(.12)					

Notes: Estimated equation (3.7) $i_t = (1-\rho)\alpha_0 + \alpha_1(1-\rho)E_t\pi_{t+k} + \lambda(1-\rho)E_t\pi_{t+k} \cdot D_{IT} + \alpha_2(1-\rho)E_t(\Delta y_{t+k}) + \rho i_{t-1} + \nu_t$ based on the Newey-West estimator; values in parentheses represent robust standard errors; $\alpha_1 > 1$ and $\alpha_1^{IT} > 1$ represents the significance level of a Chi^2 test to test whether the *Taylor-principle* holds with the null hypothesis that $\alpha_1 \leq 1$ and $\alpha_1^{IT} \leq 1$; $\alpha_1^{IT} > \alpha_1 > 1$ represents the significance level of a Chi^2 test to test whether the pre-inflation coefficient and the inflation coefficient are different with the null hypothesis that $\alpha_1^{IT} \leq \alpha_1$; $\alpha_1^{(IT)}$; * (+) indicates significance at the one (ten) percent level, respectively.

which together yields

$$(3.10) \qquad \alpha_0 = r + (1 - \alpha_1)E\pi^*.$$

This implies that

$$(3.11) \qquad E\pi^* = \frac{\alpha_0 - r}{1 - \alpha_1}$$

where $E\pi^*$ is the implicit long-term inflation rate. By the same token one can derive the implicit long-term inflation rate for the period before and after the introduction of inflation targeting:

$$(3.12) \qquad E\pi^*_{Pre} = \frac{\alpha_0^{Pre} - r^{Pre}}{1 - \alpha_1^{Pre}}; \qquad E\pi^*_{IT} = \frac{\alpha_0^{IT} - r^{IT}}{1 - \alpha_1^{IT}}$$

According to Clarida et al. (1998) we calculate the real interest rate as $r = \bar{i} - \bar{E}\pi$ where $\bar{i}$ is the average nominal interest rate over the respective period and $E\pi$ is the average of the expected inflation rate over the respective period as reported in Table 3.1. Hence, it is possible to construct the implicit long-term inflation rate before $E(\pi^*_{Pre})$ and after $E(\pi^*_{IT})$ the introduction of inflation targeting. If the introduction of inflation targeting matters for the central bank's strategy we would find that the long-term inflation rate is different between these two periods. Moreover, the comparison of the implicit long-term inflation rate for the inflation targeting period to the actual average target rate reveals whether a central bank actually follows its official inflation target rate.

Table 3.4 reports the implicit long-term inflation rate for the periods before (π^*_{Pre}) and after (π^*_{IT}) the introduction of inflation targeting and the mean of the inflation target π^{Tar}.[22] The last rows show the significance levels of several t-tests: a) and b) test whether the long-term inflation rate equals the actual inflation rate $(\pi^*_{Pre} = \pi^{Act}_{Pre}$ and $\pi^*_{IT} = \pi^{Act}_{IT})$ for both periods, c) tests whether the long-term inflation rate is the same between the two periods $(\pi^*_{Pre} = \pi^*_{IT})$. The last test d) analyzes whether the long-term inflation rate is equal to the mean of the official inflation target $(\pi^*_{IT} = \bar{\pi}^{Tar})$. While a) and b) can be interpreted as whether the central banks indeed achieved their long-term inflation rate, c) aims at analyzing the impact of the introduction of inflation targeting, and d) indicates whether a central bank actually follows its official inflation target rate.

---

[22] Note we dropped the expectation operator to keep the notation simple.

Table 3.4 reports that the long-term inflation rate is significantly lower once inflation targeting is introduced for Israel, Peru, Poland, Romania, and Turkey. Moreover, the long-term inflation rate before the introduction is very much in line with the average inflation rate reported in Table 3.1. In the case of Romania, the long-term inflation rate before (after) the introduction is 39 (5) percent while the actual inflation rate for these periods are 44 (6) percent. Also the the long-term inflation rate for the inflation targeting period of about 5 percent is significantly lower compared to the pre-inflation targeting period and is not different to the mean of the central bank's official inflation targeting rate of about 5.02. This also applies to Peru which has a long-term inflation rate of about 9 (1) percent before (in) the inflation targeting period while its average inflation rates for both periods were 12 and 1.9 percent, respectively.

Compared to this, the results for the Czech Republic, Finland, South Africa and Sweden reflect that the long-term inflation rate is not different between these two periods. Since these countries already had low inflation rates, these countries might not necessarily decrease the long-term inflation rate by means of inflation targeting introduction. Moreover, Table 3.4 shows that the implicit long-term inflation rates in these countries are very close to the actual average inflation rate for the two periods as reported in Table 3.1. For instance, for Finland (South Africa), the implicit long-term inflation rate before and after the introduction of inflation targeting of about 7.9 and 6.5 (6.5 and 6.6) percent are not statistically different from the average inflation rates prevailed in the respective period of about 4.3 and 1.2 (7.2 and 4.2) percent. Interestingly, Brazil, Chile, Colombia, Hungary, Slovakia and Spain show a relatively high variance in the estimates of the implicit long-term inflation rate. This indicates that the long-term inflation rate fluctuates during the inflation targeting period. Roger (2009) classifies inflation targeting into a disinflation and a stabilization period. While the former is characterized by substantial changes in the long-term inflation rate, the latter reflects a period of a stable long-term inflation rate. Roger (2009) reports that Brazil, Colombia, Hungary and Slovakia have been in the disinflation period at least until 2006. This indicates that the long-term inflation rate varies over the bulk of the sample period which explains the variance for these countries. In order to relax the assumption of a constant long-term inflation rate in the next section analyzes the time-variation of the long-term inflation rate.

Table 3.4: Expected inflation targets (Eπ^*) and actual inflation rates

Period/Test	Brazil	Chile	Columbia	Czech Republic	Finland	Hungary	Israel	Mexico	New Zealand
Implied Inflation Rate (Eπ^*_{Pre})	.69 (11.70)	-9.72 (140.25)	5.61 (5.24)	10.87 (.20)	7.93 (2.92)	-45.23 (151.72)	7.41 (.75)	2.94 (19.88)	–
Implied Inflation Rate (Eπ^*_{IT})	.71 (8.34)	4.80 (0.23)	19.13 (3.27)	9.04 (5.63)	6.55 (3.63)	-57.17 (753.18)	0.58 (3.59)	26.56 (31.19)	7.86 (1.68)
Average Inflation Target ($\bar{\pi}^{Tar}$)	4.80	3.08	6.22	3.82	2.00	3.93	3.44	3.64	1.69
a) Test: $\pi^*_{Pre} = \pi^{Act}_{Pre}$	.00	.90	.01	.00	.21	.66	.00	.35	–
b) Test: $\pi^*_{IT} = \pi^{Act}_{IT}$	.43	.00	.00	.32	.14	.93	.52	.63	.00
c) Test: $\pi^*_{Pre} = \pi^*_{IT}$	.99	.00	.00	.75	.71	.99	.06	.45	–
d) Test: $\pi^*_{IT} = \bar{\pi}^{Tar}$	.62	.00	.00	.35	.21	.94	.43	.46	.00

Period/Test	Norway	Peru	Poland	Romania	Slovakia	South Africa	Spain	Sweden	Turkey
Implied Inflation Rate (Eπ^*_{Pre})	5.11 (1.48)	9.40 (4.45)	48.43 (3.56)	39.03 (14.62)	5.93 (5.48)	6.48 (1.66)	-9.58 (74.44)	5.60 (0.72)	85.45 (11.09)
Implied Inflation Rate (Eπ^*_{IT})	.26 (4.12)	.74 (2.49)	3.80 (1.41)	4.74 (2.66)	-111.02 (681.99)	6.62 (4.95)	3.13 (1.66)	5.63 (0.81)	13.08 (0.84)
Average Inflation Target ($\bar{\pi}^{Tar}$)	2.50	2.50	4.41	5.02	2.67	4.25	2.81	2.00	4.50
a) Test: $\pi^*_{Pre} = \pi^{Act}_{Pre}$	.08	.47	.00	.70	.73	.65	.84	.01	.01
b) Test: $\pi^*_{IT} = \pi^{Act}_{IT}$	.74	.64	.89	.58	.87	.63	.94	.00	.00
c) Test: $\pi^*_{Pre} = \pi^*_{IT}$	.24	.00	.00	.00	.86	.98	.00	.97	.00
d) Test: $\pi^*_{IT} = \bar{\pi}^{Tar}$	.59	.48	.67	.92	.87	.63	.85	.00	.00

Notes: Real interest rates as shown in Table 3.1; the expected long-term inflation rate is calculated by the means of (3.11) $E_t\pi^* = \frac{c_0 - r}{1 - \alpha_1}$ and the estimation results of Table 3.3; the average inflation target is the mean of the inflation target during the period of inflation targeting; due to data availability for New Zealand, we only estimated the long-term inflation rate for the inflation targeting period.

3.6   A Time-varying perspective

3.6.1   The role of time-varying inflation targets

In this section we allow the inflation target to be time-varying. Treating the long-term inflation rate as a time-variant parameter accounts for institutional changes, e.g. change in the board or the regulatory environment. Ireland (2007) and Leigh (2008) provide evidence that, indeed, the long-term inflation rate of the Fed is time-varying.

As the inflation targeting countries publicly announce their inflation targets, we now incorporate the time-variance of the official inflation target into our analysis. Figures 3.1, 3.2, and 3.3 show at substantial variation of the inflation target which is especially strong in the case of Brazil, Colombia, the Czech Republic, Hungary, Israel and Poland which changed the target on a regular basis. For other countries, like Chile, Finland, Norway and South Africa, the inflation target is relatively stable. Since we do not have information for the time-varying target before the introduction of the inflation targeting, we drop the pre-inflation targeting period for our subsequent analysis and compare the inflation coefficient to the coefficient of our analysis with the constant long-term inflation rate. If a central bank has consistently responded to its inflation target, we would find that the Taylor principle still holds. This can then be interpreted as evidence in favor of a consistent central bank strategy.

Starting from Equation (3.4) we now treat the inflation target as observable but time-varying and, thus, do not need to include it in the constant. Therefore we depart from the former specification (3.7) and estimate

$$(3.13)\quad i_t = \alpha_0(1-\rho) + \alpha_1^{IT}(1-\rho)E_t(\pi_{t+k} - \pi_t^{Tar}) + \alpha_2(1-\rho)E_t\Delta y_{t+k} + \rho i_{t-1} + \epsilon_t$$

with $\alpha_0 = \bar{i}$ and π_t^{Tar} reflects the official inflation target.

Again we start by estimating Equation (3.13) in a fixed-effects panel framework for all countries. The results reported in last two columns of Table 3.2 show that the Taylor principle holds since the inflation coefficients of about 1.83 in the fixed-effects model and 2.07 in the GMM specification are significantly higher than unity. Moreover, the output coefficient is still not different from zero. For the GMM estimation we use the same set of instruments as in Section 3.4. The Wald-test, the Hansen J statistic, the Kleinberg-Paap test and the Angrist-Pischke test are in favor of our instruments.

The estimation results for each country individually are reported in Table 3.5. For Brazil, Finland, Poland, Romania, Spain and Turkey the *Taylor principle* still holds when the time-varying inflation rate is included. Interestingly, for Sweden the inflation coefficient increased substantially and is significantly larger than unity in this specification compared to the constant long-term inflation rate. This indicates that the Riksbank, indeed, very much emphasize on its inflation target. For Chile, Colombia, the Czech Republic, Israel, Mexico, New Zealand, Norway and Slovakia the inflation coefficient is still larger than but not significantly different from unity. This reflects that these central banks respond to inflation expectations in line with the Taylor principle but they do not change consistently the real interest rate if inflation expectations exceed the inflation target.

3.6.2 The time-variance of the inflation coefficient

Since the results of our analysis indicate that inflation targeting makes the difference, i.e. changes central banks response to inflation, the question arises whether the process of acting in an inflation stabilizing manner is smooth or not. Put differently, we so far restricted the inflation coefficient to be equal before and after the introduction of inflation targeting. We now focus on the time-variation of the inflation coefficient to identify the point in time when a country actually switches to a inflation stabilizing regime. This touches upon the very relevant issue of whether the adoption of inflation targeting itself is endogenous. Countries which might already have an inflation stabilizing monetary policy rule in place might be more willing to introduce inflation targeting.

To analyze how the inflation coefficient (α_1) behaves over time we simply regress the inflation and output forecast on the interest rate depending on the years before and after the inflation targeting introduction. The time-variance of the inflation coefficient $(\alpha_{1,t})$ is based on a ten year window.[23] Figure 3.5 plots the estimates of $\alpha_{1,t}$. The shaded area reflect the 99 percent confidence interval. Figure 3.5 supports the result that the inflation coefficient is higher and above unity after the introduction of inflation targeting, i.e. the *Taylor principle holds*. Compared to that, the inflation coefficient is significantly lower than unity for the period six years ahead the introduction. Until the introduction the coefficient remains relatively stable and fluctuates

---

[23] The window length is determined by the number of observations per year. We only include those periods which have more than 100 observations across all countries.

Table 3.5: Results with the time-varying inflation target

Country	α_0	α_1^{IT}	α_2	ρ	$\alpha_1 > 1$	R^2	Obs.
	14.78*	1.79*	.01	.81*	.07	.97	92
Brazil	(3.89)	(.53)	(1.09)	(.06)			
	-1.50	3.79	-.25	.97*	.16	.99	90
Chile	(4.98)	(2.81)	(.10)	(.02)			
	2.80+	1.61+	1.17*	.88*	.26	.92	.92
Columbia	(1.79)	(.95)	(.44)	(.05)			
	-1.94	1.39*	1.44	.94*	.19	.99	67
Czech Republic	(6.39)	(.44)	(1.62)	(.03)			
	1.71+	1.63*	.66	.88*	.09	.98	71
Finland	(.76)	(.46)	(.25)	(.04)			
	-1.59	1.35*	2.08*	.85*	.12	.92	43
Hungary	(2.71)	(.29)	(.71)	(.02)			
	7.55	1.48	-1.23	.98*	.45	.98	127
Israel	(9.06)	(3.79)	(2.20)	(.01)			
	4.98	2.06	.34	.79*	.22	.78	82
Mexico	(4.57)	(1.37)	(1.46)	(.06)			
	-6.64	.09	5.36	.96*	.37	.92	59
New Zealand	(13.43)	(2.72)	(5.35)	(.03)			
	-.23	-.93	-.74	.99*	.74	.99	82
Norway	(7.45)	(1.76)	(1.10)	(.01)			
	2.04*	.30	.20+	.84*	.85	.94	72
Peru	(.80)	(.67)	(.16)	(.06)			
	13.90*	4.39*	-1.75	.93*	.00	.99	59
Poland	(3.36)	(.82)	(.66)	(.02)			
	-25.64*	2.13*	5.25*	.82*	.02	.89	18
Romania	(9.23)	(.49)	(.79)	(.06)			
	.10	.49*	.50*	.50*	.99	.74	22
Slovakia	(.50)	(.16)	(.08)	(.12)			
	12.33+	-.54	-.94	.97*	.93	.96	96
South Africa	(7.44)	(1.06)	(.1.80)	(.03)			
	15.16*	2.93*	-3.64	.92*	.00	.98	48
Spain	(3.24)	(.65)	(1.08)	(.03)			
	-5.86+	3.87*	3.90+	.96*	.00	.99	179
Sweden	(4.56)	(1.08)	(1.81)	(.01)			
	18.15+	2.13*	-1.63	.75*	.02	.88	16
Turkey	(12.05)	(.48)	(2.17)	(.18)			

Notes: Estimated equation (3.13) $i_t = \alpha_0(1 - \rho) + \alpha_1^{IT}(1 - \rho)E_t(\pi_{t+k} - \pi_t^{Tar}) + \alpha_2(1 - \rho)E_t(\Delta y_{t+k}) + \rho i_{t-1} + \epsilon_t$ based on the Newey-West estimator; values in parentheses represent robust standard errors; $\alpha_1^{IT} > 1$ represents the significance level of a Chi^2 test to test whether the *Taylor-principle* holds with the null hypothesis that $\alpha_1^{IT} \leq 1$; * (+) indicates significance at the one (ten) percent level, respectively.

around unity. After the introduction the coefficient increases gradually and is significantly greater one from the second year on. Our results thus give no support to the issue that the introduction of inflation targeting might be endogenous. In contrast, central banks change their strategy after they adopted inflation targeting. Therefore we draw the conclusion that the introduction of inflation targeting itself makes the difference. Compared to that, Figure 3.6 depicts the response of the output coefficient $\alpha_{2,t}$ over time and shows no systematic pattern. Interestingly, the variance is larger for the period before the introduction indicating that at least some countries responded to the output development.

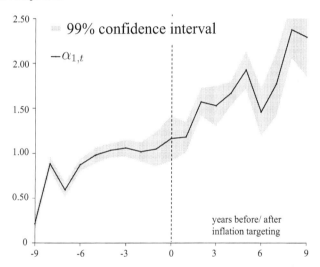

Figure 3.5: Time-varying inflation coefficient $\alpha_{1,t}$

Note: Figure 3.5 shows the time-varying inflation ($\alpha_{1,t}$) coefficient depending on the years before and after the introduction of inflation targeting ($t = 0$). The shaded area reflects the 99% confidence interval.

3.7 Conclusion

This chapter's study investigates whether the *de jure* introduction of an inflation targeting regime has changed the *de facto* central bank policy. The main contribution of this study is that we estimate the impact of the introduction of inflation targeting rather than comparing inflation and non-inflation targeting countries. Moreover, our data set is readily and frequently available to the central banks, might serve as a proxy for the future economic development and is not subject to the real time data critique. Hence, we also take into account the stylized fact, that central banks respond to the economy in a forward-looking manner.

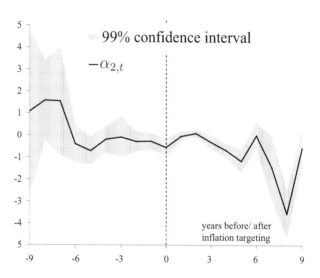

Figure 3.6: Time-varying output coefficient $\alpha_{2,t}$

Note: Figure 3.6 shows the time-varying output $(\alpha_{2,t})$ coefficient depending on the years before and after the introduction of inflation targeting $(t = 0)$. The shaded area reflects the 99% confidence interval.

This data set allows us to analyze the impact of the introduction of inflation targeting in different dimension. First, we provide evidence that compared to the pre-inflation targeting period, the majority of central banks change their willingness to fight inflation. More specifically, we find that the inflation coefficient in a standard Taylor-type rule is significantly larger (than unity) for twelve out of 18 countries once inflation targeting is introduced. However, we remain silent on whether central banks indeed successfully stabilized inflation, a topic which is been extensively discussed in the literature (Mishkin and Schmidt-Hebbel, 2006). Second, we also find that the long-term inflation rate on which monetary strategy is based, changed significantly for seven countries. Moreover, we can show that for the majority of countries the long-term inflation rate during the pre-inflation targeting period is not different to their actual average inflation rate for this period. We also find that for most countries the long-term inflation rate is consistent with its official inflation target rate. We interpret this finding as evidence that the countries are committed to their official inflation target though literature on the effectiveness of inflation targeting is mixed (Mishkin and Schmidt-Hebbel, 2006).

For Brazil, Chile, Colombia, Slovakia and Spain we found evidence that the long-term inflation rate for the inflation targeting period varies over time which confirms Ireland (2007) and Leigh (2008). Analyzing the time-variance of the inflation coefficient reveals that central banks stabilize inflation stabilizing once inflation targeting is introduced. The results provide further evidence that inflation targeting indeed makes the difference.

Chapter 4

Monetary policy and oil price expectations

4.1 Introduction

Since the beginning of the first oil crisis in October 1973, the macroeconomic effects of oil price shocks have been analyzed in detail (Carlstrom and Fuerst 2005, Natal 2009, Montoro 2010). In this regard, a large number of studies report a correlation between increases in oil prices and subsequent economic downturns (Hamilton 1983, Hamilton and Herrera 2004). However, it is not clear whether such an economic downturn is directly triggered by an oil price shock or whether the monetary policy tightening due to the inflationary pressure causes a downward movement in real economic activity. The debate on whether central banks should respond to the oil price is remarkable but contentious (Bernanke et al., 1997, Hamilton and Herrera 2004, Blanchard and Gali 2007, Svensson 2006) and there is no study examining whether central banks actually respond to the oil price. This letter tries to close this research gap and addresses the question whether central banks respond to the oil price or oil price expectations. To this end, we estimate monetary policy rules in the spirit of Taylor (1993) assuming that the short-term interest rate reacts to inflation and output. We account for the forward-looking behavior of central banks (Clarida et al., 1998, 2000) by using a unique data set of expectational data which also prevents the real-time data problem.

4.2   The data set

To estimate the central bank's reaction function, we use the relevant short-term interest rate for conducting monetary policy for the Bank of Canada (i.e., Overnight Money Market Rate), Bank of England (i.e., Overnight Inter-bank Rate), the Federal Reserve (i.e., Federal Funds Rate) and the European Central Bank (i.e., European Overnight Index Average) on a monthly basis for the time period between January 1990 and December 2007.[1] To correctly assess the information set on which the central banks base their interest rate decisions, we use inflation, GDP growth and oil price expectations (West Texas Intermediate) published monthly in the Consensus Economics Fore-cast poll.

There are several reasons of why the data set of the Consensus Economic poll is suitable to estimate monetary policy rules (Gorter et al. 2008).[2] First, the survey participants work with the private sector in the respective country[3] and hence, should report a true notion of the expected economic development. The fact that we use private sector forecasts is also of advantage compared to the forecasts of international institutions or even the central bank itself which might have an incentive to report strategic forecasts consistent with their macroeconomic policy (Batchelor 2001). Moreover, the individual forecasts are published along the name of the forecaster and its affiliation. Given that this allows everybody to evaluate the performance of the individual participants, the accuracy of the forecasts can be expected to have an effect on the reputation of the forecasters (Dovern und Weisser 2008). Second, since the poll is conducted each month during the first week and released within the second week, it is a *timely* and *frequent* dissemina-tional means for the central bank to get to know how inflation, growth and oil expectation develop. Third, the forecasts are not revised and, hence not exposed to the *real-time data critique* (Orphanides 2001).

Consensus Economics publishes the forecasts for two different time horizons, namely the current and the next year. Following Gorter et al.

---

[1]   Our sample period ends in 2007 to separate the impact of oil price shocks from the influence of the economic and financial crisis 2008-2009.

[2]   Note that for the description of the data set we heavily borrow from Rülke (2009), who used Consensus Economics data to estimate the expectation formation process in inflation targeting emerging markets economies.

[3]   The participants are professional economists working for universities and financial institutions such as international economic research institutes, investment and com-mercial banks. Further information concerning the survey can be found on the website: www.consensuseconomics.com.

(2008), Beck (2001), Heppke-Falk and Huefner (2004) we weight both forecasts with the remaining months at the time of the forecast to obtain a fixed forecast horizon of one year which is roughly the average time-lag of the monetary policy transmission.[4] In order to discriminate between the central bank's response to oil expectations and its response to inflation expectations we subtract the change in oil price expectations from the inflation expectations by using the weights attached to oil in the respective consumer basket.[5] Figure 4.1, 4.2, 4.3 and 4.4 display the short-term interest rate (solid line), the one-year-ahead inflation expectation (dotted line) and the one-year-ahead oil price forecast (fine dotted line) and shows that the volatility of expected oil price changes is much higher compared to inflation expectations.[6] Though inflation expectations and the interest rate move in line, the figure provides anecdotal evidence that central banks respond to oil price expectations. For instance, the Bank of England increased its interest rate from 6 to 7.5 percent between 1997 and 1999 although inflation expectations decreased from 3 to 2 percent. At the same time the oil price was expected to increase of about 15 percent. The Federal Reserve raised the Funds rate from 2.6 to 6 percent between 1994 and 1996 though inflation expectations remained relatively low while oil price expectations picked up.

4.3   Estimation results

Our empirical analysis is based on an oil price augmented Taylor-type rule as presented in Equation (4.1):

$$(4.1) \qquad i_t = \alpha + \alpha_\pi E_t \pi_{t+12} + \alpha_y E_t \Delta y_{t+12} + \alpha_{oil} E_t \Delta oil_{t+12} + \rho i_{t-1} + \epsilon_t$$

where i_t, ρ and ϵ refer to the interest rate, the smoothing coefficient and the error term. Moreover, $E_t \pi_{t+12}$, $E_t \Delta y_{t+12}$, and $E_t \Delta oil_{t+12}$ reflect the expected inflation, GDP growth rate[7] and oil price change. Hence, α_π (α_y)

---

[4]   See Appendix C for a detailed formula for the calculation of the weighted expectations and the relative weight of oil in the Consumer Basket.

[5]   See Appendix D for a detailed formula for calculation of the non-oil cpi.

[6]   Since stationarity is a prerequisite to estimate Taylor rules to avoid the spurious regression problem (Österholm, 2005), we tested for stationarity in our data which cannot be rejected on a one percent level.

[7]   Following Orphanides (2003), McCallum and Nelson (1999), Levin et al. (1999, 2003) and order to use a consistent data set, we use the output growth forecasts rather than the output gap. VAR based results on the output gap are similar and available upon request.

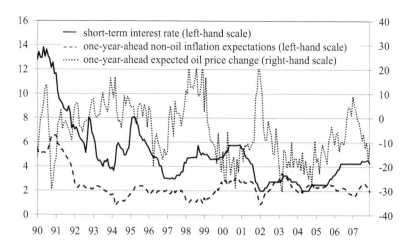

Figure 4.1: Inflation target, interest rate, expected and actual inflation rate in Canada

Note: Figure 4.1 shows the interest rate (solid line), one-year-ahead non-oil inflation expectations (dotted line) and the one-year ahead expected oil price change at time t.

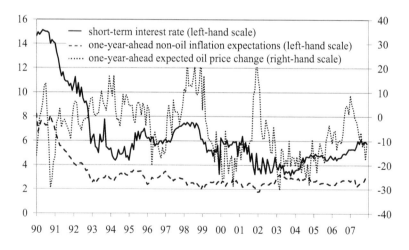

Figure 4.2: Inflation target, interest rate, expected and actual inflation rate in the UK

Note: Figure 4.2 shows the interest rate (solid line), one-year-ahead non-oil inflation expectations (dotted line) and the one-year ahead expected oil price change at time t.

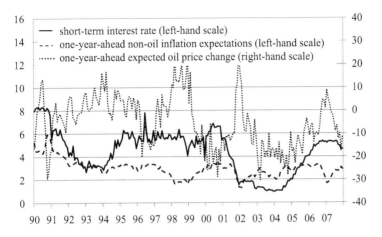

Figure 4.3: Inflation target, interest rate, expected and actual inflation rate in in the USA

Note: Figure 4.3 shows the interest rate (solid line), one-year-ahead non-oil inflation expectations (dotted line) and the one-year ahead expected oil price change at time t.

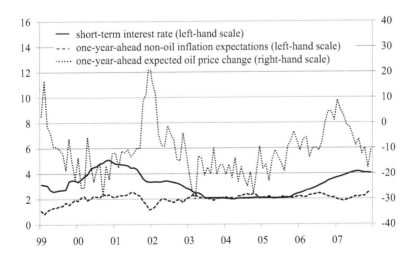

Figure 4.4: Inflation target, interest rate, expected and actual inflation rate in in the Euro Area

Note: Figure 4.4 shows the interest rate (solid line), one-year-ahead non-oil inflation expectations (dotted line) and the one-year ahead expected oil price change at time t.

and α_{oil} measure the central bank's respond to the one-year-ahead expected inflation (output) and oil price change.

Table 4.1 reports the results of Equation (4.1) for the panel setting and for each individual country based on GMM.[8] Except for the European Central Bank, the inflation coefficient is significantly higher than unity indicating that the Taylor principle holds. The output coefficient is significantly positive in the panel and for all countries, except for the UK. Interestingly, the coefficient α_{oil} is positive for all countries as well as in the panel setting. In the latter it has a magnitude of about 0.11 reflecting that a one percent increase in oil price expectations is associated with an increase in the short-term interest rate by about eleven basis points. Table 4.1 also reports that the Bank of Canada responds with a 24 basis points increase indicating substantial heterogeneity among central banks.

To account for possible asymmetries of oil price shocks (Kilian 2009), we estimated Equation (4.1) including an interaction dummy (α_{oil-}) measuring the central bank's response to expected oil price decreases while α_{oil} then reflects the response to an expected oil price increase. Column 'Asymmetry' reports that central banks rise their interest rate by about 13 basis points when oil price expectations increase by one percent. Interestingly, the response to a one percent decrease in oil price expectations is insignificant indicating an asymmetry in the central banks behavior. Additionally, we replaced the one-year-ahead oil price expectations by the one-year-ahead realized oil price. Column 'Realized' shows that central banks do not respond to the realized oil price as α_{oil} becomes insignificant. Finally, our results pass a number of diagnostic checks and robustness tests, including the Kleibergen-Paap LM-statistic, the Hansen J statistic and the Angrist-Pischke test indicating that our model is correctly identified.

4.4   Conclusion

This chapter provides robust estimates that the Bank of Canada, Bank of England, Federal Reserve and the European Central Bank respond to a one percent increase in oil price expectations with an increases in the interest rate of about eleven basis points. To correctly assess the information set of a central bank we use private sector forecasts and disentangle oil price

---

[8]   Results based on OLS, SURE and panel fixed effects are similar and available upon request.

Table 4.1: Oil augmented Taylor-type rules

Specification	Expectations	Panel Asymmetry	Realized	Bank of Canada	Bank of England	Federal Reserve	ECB
α	-	-	-	-16.29	-1.03	-9.33	-3.61
				(9.43)	(1.15)	(4.60)	(1.36)
α_π	2.06	2.06	1.86	2.98	2.06	2.44	1.25
	(.19)	(.20)	(.34)	(1.37)	(.14)	(.75)	(.71)
α_y	2.03	2.02	2.67	5.26	.45	2.58	2.63
	(.45)	(.44)	(.90)	(2.46)	(.38)	(1.03)	(.42)
α_{oil}	.11	.13	.01	.24	.05	.11	.06
	(.02)	(.04)	(.01)	(.11)	(.02)	(.06)	(.02)
α_{oil-}	-	.07	-	-	-	-	-
		(.04)					
ρ	.93	.93	.96	.96	.84	.95	.93
	(.01)	(.01)	(.01)	(.01)	(.04)	(.02)	(.02)
$\alpha_\pi > 1$	.00	.00	.00	.08	.00	.03	.36
$\alpha_y > 0$	.00	.00	.00	.02	.12	.01	.04
$\alpha_{oil} > 0$	.00	.00	.29	.02	.03	.03	.00
$\alpha_{oil-} > 0$	-	.11	-	-	-	-	-
R^2	.96	.96	.95	.99	.99	.99	.99
Obs.	742	742	742	215	215	215	107
Wald-test	.00	.00	.00	.00	.00	.00	.00
Hansen J	.43	.39	.58	.26	.25	.20	.46
K.-P.rk LM	.00	.00	.00	.05	.00	.01	.14
A.-P. χ^2							
α_π	.00	.00	.00	.00	.00	.00	.00
α_y	.00	.00	.00	.00	.00	.00	.00
α_{oil}	.00	.00	.00	.00	.00	.00	.00

Notes: Estimated Equation (4.1) $i_t = \alpha + \alpha_\pi E_t \pi_{t+12} + \alpha_y E_t \Delta y_{t+12} + \alpha_{oil} E_t \Delta oil_{t+12} + \rho i_{t-1} + \epsilon_t$; GMM estimates are based on *two-step feasible GMM* estimation with minimum asymptotic variance that are heteroscedasticity- and autocorrelation-consistent; as instruments in the panel specification we use the contemporaneous realized inflation rate as well as its first to fourth lag, the first and second lag of the inflation rate forecast, the first lag of the GDP growth forecast, the first and second lag of the oil price forecast, and the first and second lag of the real effective exchange rate; as instruments for the individual central banks we use the contemporaneous realized inflation rate as well as its first lag, the first lag of inflation rate forecast, the first lag of the GDP growth forecast, and the first lag of the oil price forecast; the null hypothesis of the Wald-test states that the instruments are weakly correlated with endogenous regressors; the Kleinbergen-Paap (K.-P.) rank LM test and the Angrist-Pischke (A.-P.) first-stage Chi^2 test are underidentification tests of whether the model is identified meaning the instruments are relevant where the null hypothesis states that the model is not identified; the Hansen J statistic tests the null hypothesis whether the instruments are uncorrelated with the error terms; for all tests we present p-values; $\alpha_\pi > 1$ represents the significance level of a Chi^2 test indicating whether the *Taylor-principle* holds with the null hypothesis that $\alpha_\pi \leq 1$; $\alpha_y > 0$ and $\alpha_{oil} > 0$ represent the significance level of a Chi^2 test on the null hypothesis whether $\alpha_y \leq 0$ and $\alpha_{oil} \leq 0$, respectively; R^2 refers to the overall coefficient of determination.

expectations from inflation expectations. We also find asymmetries in the central banks behavior and report that those central banks do not respond to realized oil price dynamics.

Chapter 5

The Euro and the Spanish housing bubble

5.1 Introduction

Spain's economic crisis starting in 2008 clearly has to be seen in the context of the world economic crisis triggered by the burst of the U.S subprime housing bubble.[1] However, especially the Spanish pre-2008 housing boom seems to originate – at least partly – east of the Atlantic Ocean. Besides governmental regulations, which for example include that 15 percent of mortgage payments are deductible from personal income, cheap credit probably played a major role for the recent housing boom in Spain. Figure 5.1 shows the development of three mortgage interest rates in Spain.[2] Whereas the average mortgage rate was between 10 and 12 percent for 1995, it dropped down to about 5 percent in 1999 and remained at a relatively low level. Additionally, Table 5.1 shows that at the same time the credit conditions were associated with a sharp increase in the volume of house purchase loans. From 1997 to 2007 the volume of house purchase loans more the sextupled from 104 Billion Euro to 645 Billion Euro. Weighted by GDP this value almost tripled form a ratio of .21 to .61.

---

[1] Bean (2009) offers an excellent overview about the causes of the financial crisis and the subsequent recession.

[2] The *'CECA' Reference Mortgage Interest Rates* is an average interest rate based on personal loans and mortgage loans provided by the Spanish Confederation of Savings Banks. The *'IRPH' Mortgage Interest Rate (Banks)* is the obtained average mortgage interest rate with a duration of more than three years offered by banks. The *'IRPH' Mortgage Interest Rate (Savings Banks)* is the obtained average mortgage interest rate with a duration of more than three years offered by savings banks.

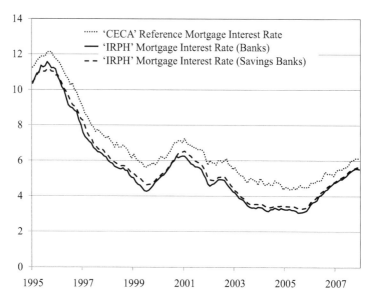

Figure 5.1: Mortgage interest rates

Note: Figure 5.1 shows the *'CECA' Reference Mortgage Interest Rates* (fine dotted line),
the *'IRPH' Mortgage Interest Rate (Banks)* (dotted line), and the *'IRPH' Mortgage Interest Rate (Savings Banks)* (solid line).

Table 5.1: House purchase loans (1997 - 2007)

Year	House purchase loans (in Billion Euro)	House purchase loans to GDP (Ratio)
1997	104	0.21
1998	126	0.23
1999	151	0.26
2000	183	0.29
2001	215	0.32
2002	250	0.34
2003	304	0.39
2004	375	0.45
2005	474	0.52
2006	570	0.58
2007	645	0.61

Source: OECD (2010).

This surge in housing demand is mirrored by a surge in house prices. Figure 5.2 shows the development of the Spanish house price index, while additionally the consumer price index (CPI) is displayed as a benchmark for comparison. Whereas the CPI increased by about 50 percent from 1995 to 2008, the house price index rocketed up by more than 200 percent.

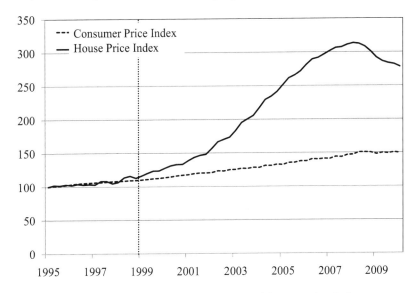

Figure 5.2: Consumer price index and house price index

Note: Figure 5.2 shows the Consumer Price Index (1995=100, dotted line) and the House Price Index (1995=100, solid line) for Spain from the first quarter of 1995 to second quarter 2010. The fine dotted vertical line indicates the date of changeover to the Euro in January 1999. The data has been taken from the OECD (2010) and the Ministerio de Viviendas (2010) in Spain, respectively.

The two indices start to drift apart around the date of the changeover to the Euro in January 1999. By this visual evidence one might be tempted to argue that with the changeover to the Euro Spain lost the ability of conducting national autonomous monetary policy and depended on the European Central Bank's monetary policy that only focuses on Euro-area wide developments. We take this claim as our motivation for analyzing the link between monetary policy and the development in Spain's real estate sector in more detail. In particular, we address the problem of the ECB's Euro-area wide one-size-fits-all monetary policy and deal with the question what would have happened if a central bank only responsible for the Spanish economy had conducted a monetary policy based on the Banco de España's pre-Euro monetary policy.

As Andrés et al. (2010) demonstrate in a DSGE model, the evolution of the Spanish economy has been remarkably different from that of the rest of the Euro Area. In particular, they find that EMU membership has had a non-negligible effect on observed growth and inflation differentials, which result from a combination of asymmetric country-specific shocks and asymmetric structure. In our study, we address the question how EMU membership (and the associated differentials in growth and inflation) affected monetary policy conditions and, moreover, focus on the consequences for the housing sector.

This chapter has the following structure. Section 5.2 briefly reviews the commonly applied empirical Taylor-type rules. Section 5.3 introduces the data set. In Section 5.4 we estimate reaction functions in the spirit of Taylor (1993) and Clarida et al. (1998) to analyze the Banco de España's pre-Euro monetary policy. In Section 5.5, we turn the the ECB's monetary policy, compare this to the Banco de España's pre-Euro monetary policy and demonstrate that the ECB's monetary policy was inadequate for Spain's economy. Section 5.6 tries give a rough guide of what would have been the consequences on housing starts if an alternative interest path had been followed. Finally Section 5.7 concludes.

5.2   The empirical morphology of Taylor-type rules

All major central banks in industrial and emerging economies currently conduct monetary policy by using market-oriented instruments in order to influence the short-term interest rate. Since the seminal paper of Taylor (1993) it has virtually become a convention to describe the interest rate setting behavior of central banks in terms of monetary policy reaction functions.[3] In its plain form, the so-called Taylor rule states that the short-term interest rate, i.e., the instrument of a central bank, reacts to deviations of inflation and output from their respective target levels. Although the Taylor rule started out as an empirical exercise, there is a clear theoretical link between optimal (inflation targeting) monetary policy and Taylor rules. Among others, Svensson (1997, 2003) showed that (contemporaneous and forward-looking) Taylor

---

[3]   Note that this section heavliy borrows from Rülke (2009), who estimated Ex-ante Taylor-type rules for the G7.

rules can be derived as the explicit solution of an optimal control problem within stylized macro models.

For the purpose of empirical exercises, in a seminal paper Clarida et al. (1998) propose a specific forward-looking variant of the Taylor rule which takes into account the pre-emptive nature of monetary policy as well as interest smoothing behavior of central banks. This particular type of reaction function has become very popular in applied empirical research. Although it is still in the spirit of the Taylor rule, specifications of this type represent a modification of the original Taylor rule and, thus, the literature often refers to them as Taylor-type rules. Following Clarida et al. (1998, 2000) and Taylor (1999) the baseline forward-looking policy rule takes the form:

$$(5.1) \qquad i_t^* = \bar{i} + \alpha_\pi E_t(\pi_{t+k} - \pi^*) + \alpha_{\tilde{y}} E_t(y_{t+k} - y_{t+k}^*),$$

where i^* is the desired level of the nominal short-term interest rate, and $\bar{i}$ is its equilibrium level. The second term on the right-hand side is the expected deviation of the k-period ahead inflation rate (π) from the target rate (π^*) which is assumed to be constant over time. The third term is the expected deviation of the k-period ahead level of output (y) from its natural level (y^*), i.e., the expected output gap $E(\tilde{y})$. The coefficients α_π and $\alpha_{\tilde{y}}$ which are to be estimated represent the reaction coefficients.

The coefficient for the inflation gap, α_π, is of particular importance. In order to act in a stabilizing manner it has to be greater than unity, which is referred to as the well-known *Taylor principle*. The central bank has to react with its nominal policy rate more than one-to-one to the underlying inflation shocks in order to increase the real interest rate. If the Taylor principle does not hold, the central bank reaction leads to a declining real interest rate in the case of rising inflation which clearly is at odds with stabilization efforts.

The additional assumption of interest rate smoothing behavior implies that:

$$(5.2) \qquad i_t = (1 - \rho)i_t^* + \rho i_{t-1} + \nu_t,$$

with the parameter ρ representing the degree of interest rate smoothing (with $0 < \rho < 1$) and ν_t represents an i.i.d. exogenous random shock to the interest rate. Combining Equations (5.1) and (5.2) leads to

$$(5.3) \quad i_t = (1 - \rho)(\bar{i} + \alpha_\pi E_t(\pi_{t+k} - \pi^*) + \alpha_{\tilde{y}} E_t(y_{t+k} - y_{t+k}^*)) + \rho i_{t-1} + \nu_t$$

Equation (5.3) represents the econometric specification which is commonly used to describe central bank behavior.[4] It is reduced to the plain Taylor rule when ρ is zero and the horizon of the forward-looking behavior of the central bank, k, is also set equal to zero in econometric exercises.

The main messages generated by empirical studies focusing on central bank behavior in industrial countries can be summarized as follows. First, forward-looking specifications seem to fit the central banks' behavior better than contemporaneous versions. Here the forward-looking feature is most relevant for the inflation gap with the horizon (k) being about one year. Second, the relevance of the *Taylor principle* for stability is well demonstrated and its presence is a strong feature for most central banks. Third, the reaction coefficient for the output gap is mostly statistically significant but has a lower level compared to the inflation gap coefficient.[5] Fourth, persistence in the short-term interest rate is a strong feature found in the data. However, what is not yet clear is whether this is due to intended interest rate smoothing or whether it is due to a strong autocorrelation in the shocks upon which monetary policy reacts.[6]

Subsequently, we estimate variants of Equation (5.3) based on reported forecasts of financial market participants. We believe that for several reasons to be discussed below private forecasts on inflation and output are suitable for the estimation of forward-looking Taylor rules. Gorter et al. (2008), for example, use private sector forecasts to show that the European Central Bank is Taylor-rule based. Before we present and discuss the empirical results, the next section briefly introduces our data set.

5.3   The data set

We use inflation and output forecasts published in the survey conducted by Consensus Economics for the time period between January 1995 and Decem-

---

[4]   Since it contains expectations on the right-hand side that are not directly observable it is common to substitute them by the observed ex-post levels of the respective variables and rearrange the estimation equation into a form that contains the expectation errors of the central bank in the error term. This form is then estimated based on the General Methods of Moments.

[5]   In particular, for the output gap the literature demonstrated that it is relevant to discriminate between ex post and real-time data (Orphanides, 2001). Since we use observed expected variables in our analysis all variables are available to the central bank in real-time.

[6]   Again, since this issue is also not of a strong concern in the present study, we refer to the recent literature. See, for instance, Rudebusch (2006).

ber 2007.[7] We choose to start our sample period when Spain introduced inflation targeting. As indicated before, it is appropriate to describe the Banco de España's (inflation targeting) monetary policy by Taylor-type rules for the time period from January 1995 until the changeover to the Euro in January 1999. Our sample period ends in 2007 to avoid that our results are influenced by the world economic and financial crisis and its monetary policy reactions starting in 2008.

There are several reasons why the data set of the Consensus Economic poll should be of interest for the central bank and hence, is suitable to estimate a forward-looking monetary policy rule.[8] First, the survey participants work with the private sector in the respective country[9] and hence, should report a true notion of the expected economic development. The fact that we use private sector forecasts is also of advantage compared to the forecasts of international institutions or even the central bank itself. While the latter might have an incentive to report strategic forecasts consistent with their macroeconomic policy, the private sector should have an incentive to provide an accurate forecast rather than a strategic forecast. As a matter of fact, Batchelor (2001) shows that the Consensus Economics forecasts are less biased and more accurate in terms of mean absolute error and root mean square error compared to OECD and IMF forecasts. Moreover, the individual forecasts are published along with the names of the forecaster and their affiliation. Since analysts are bound in their survey answers by their recommendations to clients, an analyst may find it hard to justify why (s)he gave a recommendation different to the one in the survey. Given that this allows everybody to evaluate the performance of the individual participants, the accuracy of the forecasts can be expected to have an effect on the reputation of the forecasters.[10]

---

[7]   Note that for the description of the data set we heavily borrow from Rülke (2009), who used Consensus Economics data to estimate the expectation formation process in inflation targeting emerging markets economies.

[8]   Gorter et al. (2008) use the Consensus Economics poll to estimate a Taylor-type rule for the ECB. Compared to this, Bernanke and Woodford (1997) show that strict inflation targeting based on private sector forecasts is inconsistent with the existence of rational expectations equilibrium, and that policies approximating strict inflation-forecast targeting are likely to have undesirable properties.

[9]   The participants are professional economists working for universities and financial institutions such as international economic research institutes, investment and commercial banks. Further information concerning the survey can be found in the website: www.consensuseconomics.com.

[10]   Furthermore, Dovern and Weisser (2008) show that forecasters in the Consensus Economic survey provide rational forecasts.

Second, the forecasts are currently observed data that are not revised and, hence not exposed to the *real-time data critique*. Orphanides (2001) shows that it is crucial to distinguish between real-time and revised data to correctly assess the information set on which the central bank sets its interest rate decisions. In addition, because monetary policy works with a lag, effective monetary policy should focus on *forecasted* values of the goal variables, rather than the current values. Interestingly, Bernanke (2010) emphasizes these issues when analyzing the link between monetary policy and the U.S. housing bubble. Thus, our data set seems to be particular suitable for the purpose of analyzing the Spanish housing bubble. Third, the data set is consistent over the pre-Euro time period when the Banco de España was responsible for conducting monetary policy and the time period since Spain adopted the Euro in 1999. Hence, our analysis does not suffer from problems arising in different reporting standards over time.

Consensus Economics publishes forecasts for two different time horizons, namely the current and the subsequent year. We weighted the current year forecasts with the number of remaining months of the year at the time of the forecast and the subsequent year forecast with 12 minus the current year's remaining month to obtain a fixed forecast horizon of twelve months.[11] The length of the forecast horizon of twelve months can be justified by the time-lag of the monetary policy transmission which is about twelve months (George et al., 1999). This procedure is quite common in the literature (Gorter et al. 2008, Heppke-Falk and Hüffner, 2004, and Beck, 2001). To estimate the reaction function of the type (5.3), we can directly use this constructed twelve-month-ahead CPI forecast.

Since Consensus Economics only provides output growth forecasts but we need data for the output gap forecasts, $\tilde{y}_{t+12}$, further steps are necessary with respect to our output variable. To obtain the twelve-month-ahead natural output level, y_{t+12}^*, we smooth monthly data for Spain's industrial production taken from the IMF's International Financial Statistics with a Hodrick-Presott-Filter and forward the resulting time series by twelve month.[12] For the twelve-month ahead output forecast, y_{t+12}, we multiply the actual industrial production by $(1 + \Delta y)$, where Δy is the twelve-month ahead output growth forecast constructed by using Consensus Economics' GDP forecasts. By subtracting the twelve-month-ahead natural output level, y_{t+12}^*, from the twelve-month ahead output forecast, y_{t+12}, we obtain a twelve-month-ahead output gap forecast, $\tilde{y}_{t+12}$.

---

[11] See Appendix C for the concrete formula.

[12] Since we use monthly data, we use a $\lambda = 129,600$ as suggested by Ravn and Uhlig (2002).

We use two different interest rates. For the Banco de Espanã's relevant short-term interest rate for the time period from January 1995 to December 1998 we use the Spanish interbank overnight rate. For the time period since the changeover to the Euro we use the European Over Night Index Average (EONIA).

5.4 Spain's pre-Euro monetary policy

In this section we analyze Spain's monetary policy in the pre-euro period from January 1995 to December 1998. More precisely, we estimate different variants of Taylor-type rules introduced in Section 5.2. In order to arrive at a testable relationship, the unobservable terms in Equation (5.3) have to be eliminated. Since we have data for the interest rate, the expected inflation rate and the expected output gap, we only lack information on the equilibrium interest rate and the inflation target. In a first step, consistent with Clarida et al. (1998), we treat these two variables as time-invariant and aggregate both of them into the constant.[13] Thus, we rewrite Equation (5.3) as:

$$(5.4) \quad i_t = \alpha(1 - \rho) + \alpha_\pi(1 - \rho)E_t\pi_{t+12} + \alpha_{\tilde{y}}(1 - \rho)E_t\tilde{y}_{t+12} + \rho i_{t-1} + \nu_t$$

where

$$(5.5) \qquad\qquad\qquad \alpha = \bar{i} - \alpha_\pi E\pi^*$$

The first column of Table 5.2 reports results based on the generalized methods of moments (GMM) with minimum asymptotic variance that are heteroscedasticity- and autocorrelation-consistent (Baum et al., 2007). As instruments for the forecast variables we use the third, sixth, ninth and twelfth lag of the actual inflation rate, the output gap and the real effective exchange rate. The p-value of the Hansen J-static of .67 suggests that the instruments are uncorrelated with the error term, since the null cannot be rejected at a ten percent level. The inflation coefficient, α_π, is about 2.05 and significantly greater than unity. This reflects that the Banco de España increased its interest rate by 2.05 percentage points if the expected inflation rate increased by one percentage point. Hence, the real interest rate increase is approximately 1.05 percentage points. This implies that the *Taylor principle holds* during the considered time period. Moreover, the results reported

---

[13] In our subsequent analysis we will we allow for an observable time-varying inflation target.

in the first column in Table 5.2 also show that the Spanish central bank had a substantial degree of interest rate smoothing of about .63 and did not systematically respond to changes in the expected output gap, since the output gap coefficient, $\alpha_{\tilde{y}}$, is not significantly different from zero.

Table 5.2: Taylor-type rules based on the GMM estimator

Specification	constant implicit IT	time varying IT
α	.08	4.86
	(.47)	(.63)
α_π	2.05	4.14
	(.15)	.94
$\alpha_{\tilde{y}}$	-.99	-4.63
	(.68)	(3.76)
ρ	.63	.89
	(.05)	(.03)
$\alpha_\pi > 1$	.00	.00
$\alpha_{\tilde{y}} > 0$	.94	.89
R^2	.91	.89
Obs.	48	48
Hansen J statistic	.67	.50

Notes: Estimated equation (first column) (5.4) $i_t = \alpha(1-\rho) + \alpha_\pi(1-\rho)E_t\pi_{t+12} + \alpha_{\tilde{y}}(1-\rho)E_t(\tilde{y}_{t+12}) + \rho i_{t-1} + \nu_t$; estimated equation (second column) (5.6) $i_t = \alpha(1-\rho) + \alpha_\pi(1-\rho)E_t\pi_{t+12} - \pi_t^{Tar}) + \alpha_{\tilde{y}}(1-\rho)E_t(\tilde{y}_{t+12}) + \rho i_{t-1} + \nu_t$; values in parentheses represent standard errors; GMM estimates are based on *two-step feasible GMM* estimation with minimum asymptotic variance that are heteroscedasticity- and autocorrelation-consistent; as instruments for the forecast variables we use the third, sixth, ninth and twelfth lag of the actual inflation rate, the output gap and the real effective exchange rate; the Hansen J statistic tests the null hypothesis whether the instruments are uncorrelated with the error terms; for this test we present the p-values; $\alpha_\pi > 1$ represents the significance level of a Chi^2 test to test whether the *Taylor-principle* holds with the null hypothesis that $\alpha_\pi \leq 1$; $\alpha_{\tilde{y}} > 0$ represents the significance level of a Chi^2 test to test with the null hypothesis whether $\alpha_{\tilde{y}} \leq 0$; R^2 refers to the overall coefficient of determination.

We next expand the analysis and allow the inflation target to be time-varying. Since Spain adopted inflation targeting between January 1995 and December 1998, the Banco de España publicly announced inflation targets to be used in the subsequent analysis.[14] If the Banco de España consistently responded to its inflation target, we should find that the Taylor principle

---

[14]   We use the inflation targets reported in Bernanke et al. (1999). For the time period the Banco de España announced a target range, we take the average value of this range in order to obtain a point target.

still holds. This finding can then be interpreted as evidence in favor of a consistent central bank strategy.

Starting from Equation (5.4) we now treat the inflation target as observable but time-varying and, thus, do not need to include it in the constant. Therefore we depart from the former specification (5.4) and estimate

$$(5.6) \quad i_t = \alpha(1-\rho) + \alpha_\pi(1-\rho)E_t(\pi_{t+12} - \pi_t^{Tar}) + \alpha_{\tilde{y}}(1-\rho)E_t\tilde{y}_{t+12} + \rho i_{t-1} + \epsilon_t$$

with $\alpha = \bar{i}$ and π_t^{Tar} reflecting the official inflation target.

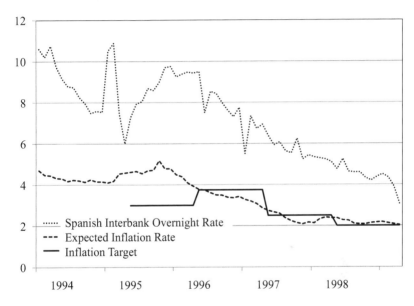

Figure 5.3: Inflation expectations and nominal interest rates

Note: Figure 5.3 shows the interest rate (fine dotted line), the expected inflation rate (dotted line), and the inflation target (solid line).

The second column of Table 5.2 reports the results based on the generalized methods of moments (GMM) with the same set of instruments as before. The Hansen J statistic of .50 again is in favor of our instruments. The inflation coefficient is about 4.86 and the p-value of .00 for the test $\alpha_\pi > 1$ again indicates that the *Taylor-principle holds*. Consistent with our estimates with a constant implicit inflation target shown in the first column of Table 5.2, the output gap coefficient is still not significantly different from zero. However, the interest rate smoothing parameter is now higher.

For an illustration Figure 5.3 shows the Spanish interbank overnight rate, the expected inflation rate, π_{t+12}, and the inflation targets announced by the Banco de España. Whereas the interest rate fall from about 8 percent in January 1995 to about 3 percent in December 1998, the inflation expectations only fall disproportionately from about 4.5 percent to about 3 percent. Thus, one could be temped to draw the conclusion that our findings do not really reflect an inflation stabilizing monetary policy, since there was no need to increase policy rates during the considered time period. However, in the first half of 1995 a rise in inflation expectation provoked the Banco de España to an aggressive rise of the interest rate. Moreover, in times when inflation expectations lie above the inflation target (1995 and beginning of 1998), the interest rate tends to increase and in times when inflation expectations lie below the inflation target (1996 and 1997), the interest rate tends to decrease.

We take this section's results as strong evidence that the Banco de España followed an inflation stabilizing monetary policy in the time period before the changeover to the Euro from January 1995 to December 1998. This result confirms the findings in Chapter 3 where we also estimate Taylor-type rules with constant long term inflation target and time-varying inflation targets for Spain by using Consensus Economics forecast data. However, the approach in Chapter 3 is somewhat different since we use output growth rate forecasts instead of a forward-looking output gap and, moreover, we there applied a Newey-West estimator instead of a GMM estimator.

5.5   Monetary policy after the Euro

We will now use the estimation results of the previous section to construct a hypothetical interest rate that potentially could have prevailed in Spain since 1999 if a central bank only responsible for the Spanish economy had followed a monetary policy based on the Banco de España's pre-Euro monetary policy during the inflation targeting period form January 1995 to December 1998.

To do so, we calibrate the Taylor-type Rule given by (5.4) with the point estimates from the first column of Table 5.2. Thus, we take $\alpha_\pi = 2.05$ and $\alpha_{\tilde{y}} = 0.00$, since the output gap parameter is not significantly different from zero. The constant can be calculated by $\alpha = \bar{i} - \alpha_\pi E\pi^*$. The average of the interest rate for the time period 1999 to 2007 is given by $\bar{i} = 3.08$. For the inflation target we use $\pi^* = 2$, which was the last inflation target announced by the Banco de España's for the year 1998 and, moreover, also reflects the ECB's objective to keep inflation below, but close to two percent. Consequently, the constant is given by $\alpha = -1.02.$[15] The interest rate smoothing parameter is set equal to $\rho = .63$. The inflation forecasts, π_{t+12}, is based on Consensus Economics forecast data for the Spanish economy for the time period of January 1999 to December 2007.[16]

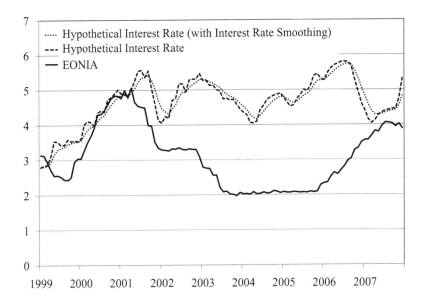

Figure 5.4: EONIA and hypothetical interest rate

Note: The fine dotted line in Figure 5.4 shows a *Hypothetical Interest Rate (with interest rate smoothing)* based on (5.4) $i_t = (1 - \rho)\alpha + \alpha_\pi(1 - \rho)E_t\pi_{t+12} + \alpha_{\tilde{y}}(1 - \rho)E_t(\tilde{y}_{t+12}) + \rho i_{t-1} + \nu_t$ with $\alpha = -1.02$, $\alpha_\pi = 2.05$, $\alpha_{\tilde{y}} = 0.00$, and $\rho = .63$ reflecting the Banco de España's pre-Euro monetary policy. The dotted line show the *Hypothetical Interest Rate*, but without interest rate smoothing – that is $\rho = .00$. The solid line shows the Euro OverNight Index Average (EONIA).

The fine dotted line in Figure 5.4 shows the hypothetical interest rate obtained by the described procedure. We also calculate a hypothetical

---

[15] As an alternative we also used our estimate for the constant shown in the first column of Table 5.2. This would imply $\alpha = .00$, since the reported value is not significantly different from zero. However, we do not decide for this option, because $\alpha = -1.02$ can be interpreted as the more *defensive* estimate as will become clearer in the subsequent analysis.

[16] Note that we do not need any output gap forecasts, since the output gap coefficient is zero.

interest rate without interest rate smoothing (that is $\rho = .00$) given by the dotted line. However, this does not change our results noticeably. Figure 5.4 also shows the actual interest rate (i.e. EONIA) that prevailed during the considered time period. As can be seen from the figure, the EONIA never really exceeds the hypothetical interest rate. However, from 1999 until the end of 2001 the hypothetical and actual interest rates do not differ by more than about one percent and move quite jointly. In contrast to this, since 2002 the interest rates drifted apart. Whereas our hypothetical interest rate fluctuates between 4 and 6 percent, the EONIA falls to about 2 percent until the middle of 2003 and, subsequently, remains at this level for two and a half years. Interestingly, the growth of the gap between the house price index and the consumer price index shown in Figure 5.2 exactly accelerates from this date on. In the second half of 2005 the gap between the EONIA and the hypothetical interest rate reached its peak with an interest rate differential of about 3.5 percentage points.

Figure 5.5 shows the spread between interest rates implied by different Taylor-type rules and the EONIA. The solid line gives the difference between the interest rate implied by the Taylor-type rule with constant implicit inflation target and the EONIA, both shown in Figure 5.4. This difference can be interpreted as a measure of the inadequacy of the actual interest rate (EONIA). The dotted line depicts the spread which we would obtain by using the Taylor-type rule with the officially announced time-varying inflation targets shown in the second column of Table 5.2. As can be seen, this would imply an even higher degree of inadequacy of the EONIA. Compared to this the fine dotted line shows the difference between the interest rate based on Taylor's (1993) original rule[17] and the EONIA. This measure is also used by Bean (2009) to show the inappropriateness of the U.S. Federal Funds Rate before the financial crisis. Interestingly, our two alternative measures based on the Banco de España pre-Euro monetary policy move quite jointly with the one based on Taylor's original rule.

Interestingly, our findings are in contrast to those for the U.S.. Whereas the interest rate path under Taylor's (1993) original rule with actual inflation rate and output gap is about 200 basis points above the target federal fund

---

[17]   Note that the original Taylor rule implies values of $\pi^* = 2.00$, $\alpha_\pi = 1.50$, $\alpha_{\tilde{y}} = .50$, and $\rho = .00$. Moreover, we replaced the expected inflation rate and the expected output gap by the actual inflation rate and the actual output gap. We also calibrated Taylor's original rule with our expectational data and found a slightly different interest path. However, it never falls below the interest rate path based on a Taylor Type Rule with constant implicit target given by the solid line in Figure 5.5. Hence, the main massage remains unchanged.

rate between 2002 and 2006, the interest rate path under a Taylor rule based on forecasts that were actually made in real-time does not differ notably from the target federal fund rate (Bernanke (2010), Dokko et al. (2009)). Put differently, the Fed's monetary policy cannot be described as too expansionary if one takes the real-time information set as a basis for evaluation. In contrast to this, our findings for the Spain are robust to alternative rules based on forecasts and suggest that the interest path set by the ECB was too expansionary for the Spanish economy.

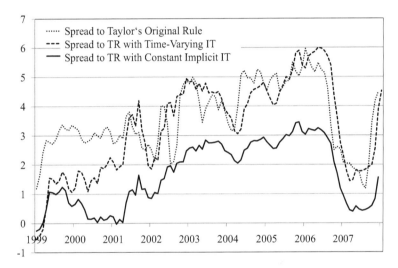

Figure 5.5: Spread between interest rates implied by different Taylor rules and the EONIA

Note: Figure 5.5 shows the spreads between interest rates implied by different Taylor rules and the EONIA. The fine dotted line illustrates the spread between the interest rate based on Taylor's (1993) original rule and the EONIA. The dotted line is based on the interest rate obtained from a Taylor Type Rule with a time-varying inflation target and without interest rate smoothing (second column of Table 5.2). The solid line is based on the interest rate obtained from a Taylor Type Rule with a constant implicit inflation target and without interest rate smoothing (first column of Table 5.2).

At this point of the analysis we would like to clearly point out the limits of our approach and advise against deducing any wrong conclusions from our results. It is important to be aware that our results are based on a very strong *ceteris paribus* assumption. Our analysis assumes that potentially higher inflation rates would not have influenced future expectations for the inflation rate nor the output gap. That is, we do not incorporate the fact that alternative interest rates would have influenced the values of the expected inflation rate and the expected output gap. For example, a potentially higher interest rate in a certain point of time probably would have been associated with lower expected inflation rates and these lower expected inflation rates, in turn, would have been associated with a lower interest rate path. As a result, it is not possible to interpret the hypothetical interest rate as an interest rate that really would have prevailed if a central bank responsible for the Spanish economy would have followed the Banco de España's pre-Euro monetary policy from 1999 to 2007. In contrast, what the hypothetical interest rate really shows is how the interest rate would have been set if in a certain point of time a switching from the actual ECB monetary policy to the Banco de Espanã's pre-Euro monetary policy would have taken place.

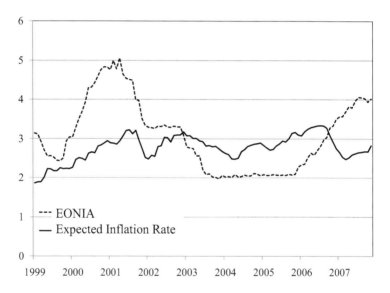

Figure 5.6: Inflation expectations and nominal interest rates

Note: Figure 5.6 shows the interest rate (fine dotted line), the expected inflation rate (dotted line), and the inflation target (solid line).

As an interesting experiment we estimated equation (5.4) with the EONIA as the short-term interest rate and the expected inflation rate and the expected output gap for Spain for the Euro time period from 1999 to 2007. Not surprisingly, we do not obtain an inflation coefficient (significantly)

greater than one. Hence, the Taylor principle does not hold.[18] As a consequence, increasing inflation expectations were associated with a fall in Spain's real interest rate. Put differently, the ECB's monetary policy clearly had an inflation *destabilizing* impact on Spain's economy. For illustration Figure 5.6 shows the EONIA and the expected inflation rate. In particular between 2002 and 2006 increasing inflation expectations are not offset by interest rate increases as the Taylor principle would have called for.

As Bernanke (2010) points out, a Taylor rule-based description of monetary policy is subject to a number of limitations. First, Taylor rules are only rules of thumb and there is disagreement about important detail regarding the construction of such rules. Second, many relevant factors are left out, for example the consideration of the zero lower bound. Another relevant issue, in particular for this chapter, is that the interest rate is not related to any asset price variables reflecting developments in the real estate sector. As a consequence, even advocates of Taylor rules point out that these rules are not a substitute for a more complete monetary policy analysis and should be used only as guidelines. However, although we keep in mind this limitations, our analysis provides evidence that the ECB's monetary policy was too expansionary for the Spanish economy.

5.6 Consequences for the housing sector

We now analyze the implications of the ECB's monetary policy for Spain's real estate sector. We start by considering the mortgage real interest rate, which can be obtained by subtracting the expected inflation rate from the 'IRPH' mortgage interest rate for banks from Figure 5.1. The resulting mortgage real interest rate is shown in Figure 5.7 for the time period from January 1999 to December 2007. Whereas in the beginning of 2001 the mortgage real interest rate lies above 3 percent, it falls under 1 percent within the subsequent two years. From the beginning of 2003 to the end of 2005 it remains below 1 percent, where a value of slightly less then 0 percent in October 2005 marks its lowest level. Thus, during this three year time period it was possible to borrow money for buying real estate property at (nearly) no real costs.

As an additional exercise Figure 5.7 also shows an additional hypothetical mortgage real interest rate that we obtained by adding the differential

---

[18]   Regression results are not reported here, but are available upon request.

between the hypothetical interest rate and the EONIA from Figure 5.4 to the real mortgage rate. This hypothetical mortgage real interest rate again reflecting our "what if the Spanish Central Bank were still in place-scenario" is relatively stable during the entire time period and fluctuates between 2.7 and 3.9 percent. Between 2001 and 2002 the gap between the hypothetical and the actual mortgage real interest rate opens from 0 percent to more than 2 percentage points. Between 2003 and 2005 the gap was always greater than 2 percentage points. In the second half of 2005 it even exceeded 3 percentage points.[19] The usage of our alternative measures of the inadequacy of monetary policy from Figure 5.5 would have implied an even higher hypothetical mortgage real interest rate.

Figure 5.7: Actual and hypothetical mortgage real interest rate

Note:The Solid line of Figure 5.7 shows a Mortgage Real Interest Rate obtained by subtracting the expected inflation rate from the 'IRPH' Mortgage Interest Rate (Banks). The dotted line represents a Hypothetical Mortgage Real Interest Rate, which obtained by adding the Spread to the Taylor rule with constant implicit inflation target of Figure 5.7 to the Mortgage Real Interest Rate.

---

[19]   We remind the reader of the ceteris paribus assumption concerning the interdependence of different variables (see Section 5.5) and therefore caution against misinterpreting the hypothetical mortgage real interest rate.

An interesting question that arises is "what would have happened in the housing sector if an alternative path for the monetary policy rate described by our 'hypothetical' interest rates was followed". We, therefore, follow an approach suggested by Taylor (2007) and estimate an equation with housing starts taken from the Spanish National Statistic Institute (INE)[20] on the left hand side and the monetary policy rate as the explanatory variable on the right hand side. We estimate the equation with monthly data from January 1990 to December 2007. The result presented in Table 5.3 shows a strong significant effect of the monetary policy rate upon housing starts with a lag of one year.[21]

Table 5.3: Estimates for housing equation

constant	16,688.10
	(867.91)
$\alpha_{i_{t-12}}$	-799.645
	(94.24)
observations	204
R^2	0.68

Notes: Estimated equation $housing starts = constant + \alpha_{i_{t-12}} i_{t-12}$ based on Newey-West estimator, where $housing starts$ represents the number of given building licenses and i_{t-12} give the one year lag of the relevant monetary policy rate; values in parentheses represent standard errors; R^2 refers to the overall coefficient of determination.

We use this result to simulate housing starts for the time period from January 1999 to 2007 with two different interest rates. The implied housing starts are shown in Figure 5.8. The small dotted line shows simulated housing starts, when we use the actually observed monetary policy rate, i.e. the EONIA. Between 1999 and 2004, this simulation seems to fit the trend in actual housing starts (solid line) quite well. However, between 2005 and 2007 the difference between the simulation and actual housing starts to diverge. The ongoing rise in house prices (see Figure 5.2) might serve as an explanation for this. At some point, buyers became more and more convinced that house prices would only go up. As a consequence, the expected value enhancement of real estate property increased which, in turn, drove up housing starts.[22]

---

[20] In fact, the INE reports the given building licenses by the Spanish authorities, which we use as approximation for housing starts.

[21] We also tried alternative lags or the contemporaneous monetary policy rate, but obtained the best fit for a lag of one year.

[22] As suggested by Taylor (2007), we also estimate our housing equation with the lagged

Moreover, the very low *real* interest rates (see Figure 5.7) – that are more relevant to determine credit conditions – might give a further explanation why simulated housing starts and actual housing starts diverged since 2005.[23] In addition to that, psychological factors still seem to have played a role.

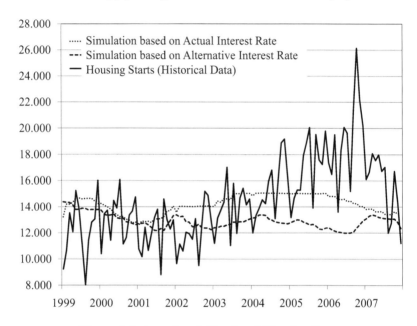

Figure 5.8: Actual and Simulated Housing Starts

Note: Figure 5.8 shows housing starts based on a simulation with the actual interest rate (fine dotted line), housing starts based on a simulation with the an alternative interest rate (dotted line) – that is the Hypothetical interest rate without smoothing of Figure 5.4 and the actual housing starts (solid line) based on given building licenses of the Spanish authorities.

Compared to this, a simulation based on our hypothetical interest rate from Figure 5.4 departs from the simulation based on the EONIA and

---

house price inflation as an additional explanatory variable. We find that house price inflation has a significantly positive effect on housing starts. Moreover, the adjusted R^2 also increases indicating that more of the variation in housing starts is explained. Under this specification, actual housing starts fit quite well simulated housing starts based on the EONIA and the actual house price inflation.

[23] As we will discuss in a moment, *real* interest rates indeed explain more of the overall variation in housing starts than *nominal* interest rates.

implies 1,500 to 3,000 housing starts less per month between 2002 and 2006. For the entire time period from 1999 to 2007 our simulation implies about 130,000 housing starts less, which is an 8 percent share of observed housing starts. A more restrictive interest rate path would have avoided much of the Spanish housing boom. Note that our alternative Taylor rules (with a time-varying inflation target or Taylor's original rule) would even suggest greater differences for the housing starts, since the implied interest rates would have been even more restrictive. In addition to this, we used the real mortgage interest rate from Figure 5.7 instead of the EONIA in the housing equation. We obtained a slightly better goodness-of-fit measure for the model and very similar results. However, since the real mortgage rate is not directly controllable by the central bank, our simulation based on the monetary policy rate is more adequate for the purpose of this study.

This section's results can be taken as a prime example for an asymmetric monetary policy effect as discussed in Baldwin and Wyplosz (2009, pp. 512 - 513). As demonstrated by different authors the ECB's monetary policy is Taylor rule-based for the aggregate Euro-area as a whole (Bean (2009), Gorter et al. (2008)), but this on average adequate (nominal) interest rate path was too expansionary for the Spanish economy. The associated increase in expected inflation rates (and also actual inflation rates) brought further down (mortgage) real interest rates and thus played an important role for the boom in Spain's real estate sector. As our simulation suggests much of the trouble in the real estate sector could have been avoided if the interest rate followed a different path.

5.7 Conclusion

Based on a Taylor-type rule this chapter investigates the Banco de España's monetary policy before the changeover to the Euro. Using this result, we demonstrate how the interest rate in the Euro period would have been set if a central bank exclusively responsible for the Spanish economy was able to continue the Banco de Españã's pre-Euro monetary policy. Comparing this to the actually observed path of the short-term interest rate (EONIA) we come to the conclusion that the ECB's monetary policy was too expansionary for Spain's economy contributing much to the trouble in the Spanish housing sector.

Our analysis can be taken as an example for an asymmetric monetary policy effect and reflects the "one-size-fits-all" problem of monetary union membership: In case of heterogeneous economic developments among the member states, it is impossible for the central bank to conduct an appropriate monetary policy for all members. Hence, the conclusion we draw is that the *burst* of Spain's housing bubble might be associated with the world economic crisis, but that the *appearance* of the bubble is caused by an inadequate monetary policy for Spain's economy, which in turn is closely linked to Spain's EMU membership.

Chapter 6

Conclusion and policy implications

This thesis deals with the empirical application of monetary policy rules based on survey data. It focused on a specific class of empirical reaction functions - often referred to as Taylor-type rules - where the interest rate is related to deviations of inflation and output from their respective target levels. Since a forward-looking variant of this policy rule with interest rate smoothing according to Clarida et. al (1998, 2000) is the the most popular one, this thesis also follows this direction. The utilized survey data set about expectational data provided by Consensus Economics turns out to be in particular suitable for the purpose of estimating forward-looking reaction functions, since the forecasts of this data set are currently observed data which are not revised and, hence are not subject to the *real-time data critique* by Orpahanides (2001).

Chapter 2 provides a theoretical foundation of the Taylor principle – the nominal interest rate should be adjusted by more than one-for-one with changes in the inflation rate (Bullard and Mitra (2002))– which is often used as a guideline for sound monetary policy. However, the Taylor principle gives only a rough guide of how to adjust the interest rate. As has been demonstrated, the response to changes in the output gap is also of importance. Moreover, this chapter demonstrated that the critical values of how the nominal interest rate has to be adjusted to changes in the inflation rate and the output gap for a stable equilibrium heavily depend on the specific calibration. Although this observation does not alter the results qualitatively and thus do not seem to be of great importance for economic theory, it can be highly relevant when it comes to the evaluation of empirical studies. Equipped with this result, Chapter 3, Chapter 4, and Chapter 5 discuss three different studies of how econometric evaluation of monetary policy based on Taylor-type rules can be conducted.

Chapter 3 offers a Taylor rule based analysis of the introduction of inflation targeting. It provides evidence that the introduction of inflation targeting changes central banks' monetary policy reaction functions. The inflation coefficient in a forward-looking Taylor-type rule is significantly larger (than unity) for twelve out of 18 considered countries once inflation targeting is introduced. Moreover, an analysis regarding the development of the inflation reaction function over time indicates that after the introduction of inflation targeting the coefficient increases gradually and is significantly greater than one from the second year on. This result thus gives no support to the issue that the introduction of inflation targeting might be endogenous. In contrast, central banks change their strategy after they adopted inflation targeting. Thus, the introduction of inflation targeting itself makes the difference.

Chapter 4 considers oil price expectations in an oil price augmented forward-looking Taylor-type rule and provides robust estimates that the Bank of Canada, Bank of England, Federal Reserve and the European Central Bank respond to oil price expectations. Interestingly, these central banks do not respond to the realized oil price. Moreover, this chapter finds asymmetries in the central banks behavior. Whereas they rise their interest rate when oil price expectations increase, the response to a decrease in oil price expectations is insignificant.

Chapter 5 estimates forward-looking reaction functions in the spirit of Taylor (1993) to investigate Spain's monetary policy conditions before and after the changeover to the Euro. Whereas the Banco de España's pre-Euro monetary policy was clearly inflation stabilizing, the ECB's monetary policy since 1999 was too expansionary for Spain's economy. This result is linked to the developments in Spain's housing sector and suggest that much of the trouble in Spain's housing sector could have been avoided by conducting a monetary policy based on the Banco España's pre-Euro monetary policy. Consequently, this chapter's analysis can be taken as a prime example for an asymmetric monetary policy effect and the associated "one-size-fits-all" problem of monetary union membership: In case of heterogeneous economic developments among the member states, it is impossible for the central bank to conduct an appropriate monetary policy for all members.

This thesis comes to the following two main conclusions. First, forward-looking Taylor-type rules are well suited to be applied to the real world. The three Taylor rule based studies in Chapter 3, Chapter 4, and Chapter 5 adressed quite different questions about monetary policy. All of them are of high practical relevance. Second, macroeconomic performance has been better when central bank decisions are based on such rules. In particular Chapter 5 suggests that a non-Taylor principle based monetary policy is associated with Spain's problems in the housing sector. Moreover, Chapter 3 demonstrates that the introduction of inflation targeting is associated with the fulfillment of the Taylor principle, which in turn stabilzes inflation.[1]

Finally, it is important to caution against the mistake of taking the word *rule* literally. As emphasized by many economists, Taylor-type rules should not be interpreted as mechanic rules. Other factors not included in the policy rule – such as for example the risk of the policy rate hitting the zero lower bound (Bernanke, 2010) – have to be taken into account. Consequently, as also stated by Bernanke (2010), Taylor-type rules do not serve as a substitute for a complete monetary policy analysis and should be used only as a *guideline* for sound monetary policy.

---

[1] As Taylor and Williams (2010) state, these two results hold for a wide range of studies regarding Taylor type rules. Thus, this dissertation provides further support for their findings.

Appendix A

Determinacy of a forward-looking Taylor rule

We have to transform (2.12) into the form given by (2.5). Thus we premultiply both sides of (2.12) with the inverse of A_1:

$$(\text{A.1}) \qquad \begin{bmatrix} x_t \\ \pi_t \end{bmatrix} = A \begin{bmatrix} E_t x_{t+1} \\ E_t \pi_{t+1} \end{bmatrix} + [A_1]^{-1} \mathbf{v}_t,$$

where $A = [A_1]^{-1} A_2 = \begin{bmatrix} 1 - \varphi \phi_x & \varphi(1 - \phi_\pi) \\ \kappa(1 - \varphi \phi_x) & \beta + \kappa \varphi(1 - \phi_\pi) \end{bmatrix}$ is the relevant matrix for determinacy. Because both the inflation rate, π_t, and the output gap, x_t, depend on their expectations formed at date t, we have two non-predetermined variables (see definition 2). Thus, we need both eigenvalues of A to be inside the unit circle (i.e. to have moduli strictly less than 1) for uniqueness. To obtain the eigenvalues, λ_i, of A we have to consider the characteristic polynomial which is for 2 x 2 matrices in general given by:

$$(\text{A.2}) \qquad |\lambda I - A| = \lambda^2 - tr(A)\lambda + det(A),$$

where $det(A) = \beta(1 - \varphi \phi_x)$ and $-tr(A) = \kappa \varphi(\phi_\pi - 1) + \varphi \phi_x - 1 - \beta$. According to Bullard and Mitra (2002), both eigenvalues of A are inside the unit circle if and only if the following conditions hold (LaSalle, 1986, p. 28):

$$(\text{A.3}) \qquad |det(A)| < 1,$$

(A.4) $|tr(A)| < 1 + det(A).$

From $(A.3)$ follows inequality (2.13) and from $(A.4)$ we obtain inequalities implies (2.14) and (2.15). Thus we arrive at *proposition 1.*

Appendix B

E-Stability of a Forward-Looking Taylor Rule

In a first step we derive the *minimal state variable* (MSV) solution (McCallum, 1983) for the system of difference equations $(A.1)$ for the REE by using the method of undetermined coefficients. With $\mathbf{y} = \begin{pmatrix} x_t & \pi_t \end{pmatrix}'$ and $B = [A_1]^{-1}$ we rewrite $(A.1)$ as

$$(\text{B.1}) \qquad\qquad \mathbf{y}_t = AE_t\mathbf{y}_{t+1} + B\mathbf{v}_t.$$

We guess a solution of the form

$$(\text{B.2}) \qquad\qquad \mathbf{y}_t = \bar{c}\mathbf{v}_t,$$

where $\bar{c}$ is a 2 x 2 matrix that has to be determined. Because of $(B.1)$ and (2.3) and (2.4) we can set up the following conditions

$$(\text{B.3}) \qquad\qquad E_t\mathbf{y}_t = \bar{c}\mathbf{v}_t,$$

$$(\text{B.4}) \qquad\qquad E_t\mathbf{y}_{t+1} = \bar{c}\mathbf{v}_{t+1} = \bar{c}F\mathbf{v}_t = F\mathbf{y}_t.$$

Plugging $(B.4)$ into $(B.1)$ and rearranging gives

$$(\text{B.5}) \qquad\qquad \mathbf{y}_t = (I - FA)^{-1}B\mathbf{v}_t,$$

where I denotes a 2 x 2 identity matrix. It is easy to see that with $\bar{c} = (I - FA)^{-1}B$, (2.34) gives the MSV solution for the REE.

Suppose the PLM is given by

(B.6) $$\mathbf{y}_t = a + c\mathbf{v}_t.$$

Note that we allow for a structural deviation of (B.6) from the MSV solution for the REE (B.2) in form of an intercept $a \neq 0$. Moreover, it is possible that $c \neq \bar{c}$. Based on the PLM economic agents form their expectations according to

(B.7) $$E_t^* \mathbf{y}_{t+1} = a + cF\mathbf{v}_t.$$

Plugging (B.7) into (B.1) gives the ALM

(B.8) $$\mathbf{y}_t = Aa + (AcF + B)\mathbf{v}_t.$$

Now we can carry out the *mapping* from the PLM (B.6) to the ALM (B.8):

(B.9) $$T\begin{pmatrix} a \\ c \end{pmatrix} = \begin{pmatrix} Aa \\ AcF + B \end{pmatrix}.$$

To obtain the conditions for E-stability we set up the following differential equation:

$$\frac{d}{d\tau}\begin{pmatrix} a \\ c \end{pmatrix} = T\begin{pmatrix} a \\ c \end{pmatrix} - \begin{pmatrix} a \\ c \end{pmatrix}$$

(B.10) $$= \begin{pmatrix} Aa \\ AcF \end{pmatrix} - \begin{pmatrix} a \\ c \end{pmatrix}$$

$$= \begin{pmatrix} 0 \\ B \end{pmatrix} + \begin{pmatrix} (A - I)a \\ (FA - I)c \end{pmatrix}.$$

According to theorem 5 the difference equation (B.10) is globally asymptotical stable if (i) both eigenvalues of the matrix $(A - I)$ have negative real parts and (ii) if both eigenvalues of matrix $((FA - I))$ have negative real parts. Note that condition (i) is equivalent to the condition that both eigenvalues of matrix A have real parts less than one. Moreover, condition (ii) is satisfied if the product of the eigenvalues A and F have real parts less that one. Because $0 \leq \mu <1$ and $0 \leq \rho <1$ both eigenvalues of F have real parts less than one. Thus it is sufficient to have both eigenvalues of A to have real parts less than one to satisfy condition (i) and (ii).

According to Bullard and Mitra (2002), both eigenvalues of A have real parts less than one (i.e. both eigenvalues of $(A-I)$ have negative real parts) if

(B.11) $$tr(A - I) < 0,$$

and

(B.12) $$det(A - I) > 0.$$

From $(A - I)$ we obtain $tr(A - I) = -(\frac{1-\beta}{\varphi} + (\phi_\pi - 1)\kappa + \phi_x)$ and $det(A - I) = (\phi_\pi - 1)\kappa\varphi + (1 - \beta)\phi_x\varphi$. Because $(B.12)$ implies $(B.11)$ we can formulate *Proposition 2*.

Appendix C

Weighted average of expected GDP and CPI

In order to generate a forecast f_t with a twelve-month forecast horizon, we calculated a weighted arithmetic average of the forecast for the current year f_t^{cur} and the next year f_t^{next}. We weight the forecast f_t with the remaining number of months m (with 1 ($=$ December) $\leq$ m $\leq$ 12 ($=$ January)) at the time of the forecast t (Rülke (2009)). The twelve-month GDP and CPI forecasts f_t are as follows:

$$(C.1) \qquad f_t = \frac{f_t^{cur} \cdot m + (12 - m) \cdot f_t^{next}}{12}$$

This procedure is also applied by Gorter et al. (2008), Heppke-Falk and Hüffner (2004) and Beck (2001). All studies deal with data of the Consensus Economic Forecast poll and construct the arithmetic average as outlined above.

Appendix D

Calculation of the non-oil CPI

Since inflation expectations consist of oil price expectations, we use the weights of oil prices in the consumer basket (γ) reported by the respective central bank and shown in Table $D.1$. Since the weights do not change noticeably over time and in order to isolate the effect of oil price expectations from time-varying compositions of the consumer basket we used constant weights. We split the overall inflation expectation $E_t\pi_{t+12}$ into the unobservable non-oil inflation expectations $E_t\widehat{\pi_{t+12}}$ by means of the observable oil price expectation $E_t\Delta oil_{t+12}$:

$$\text{(D.1)} \qquad E_t\pi_{t+12} = (1-\gamma) \cdot E_t\widehat{\pi_{t+12}} + \gamma \cdot E_t\Delta oil_{t+12}$$

which can be rearranged to

$$\text{(D.2)} \qquad E_t\widehat{\pi_{t+12}} = \frac{E_t\pi_{t+12} - \gamma \cdot E_t\Delta oil_{t+12}}{1-\gamma}$$

where $E_t\widehat{\pi_{t+12}}$ reflects the unobservable non-oil inflation expectation.

Table D.1: Relative weight (γ) of oil in the consumer basket

Country	Canada	UK	U.S.	Euro-Area
Weights (in percent)	2.0	1.8	2.1	1.7

Source: Bank of Canada, Bank of England, Federal Reserve and European Central Bank.

Bibliography

Andrés, Javier, Samuel Hurtado, Eva Ortega, and Carlos Thomas (2010), Spain in the Euro: a general equilibrium analysis, *Journal of the Spanish Economic Association* 1 (1-2), pp. 67-95.

Baldwin, Richard and Charles Wyplosz (2009), The Economics of European Integration, Third Edition, McGraw-Hill.

Ball, Lawrence M. (1998), Policy Rules for Open Economies, Research Discussion Paper No.9806, Reserve Bank of Australia.

Batchelor, Roy A. (2001), How useful are the Forecasts of Intergovernmental Agencies? The IMF and OECD versus the Consensus, *Applied Economics* 33 (2), pp. 225-235.

Baum, Christopher F., Mark E. Schaffer, and Steven Stillmann (2007), Enhanced Routines for Instrumental/ GMM Estimation and Testing, Boston College Working Paper No. 667.

Bean, Charles (2009), The Great Moderation, the Great Panic and the Great Contraction, *Journal of the European Economic Association* 8(2-3), 289-325.

Beck, Roland (2001), Do Country Fundamentals Explain Emerging Market Bond Spreads?, Discussion Paper No. 2001/02, Center for Financial Studies.

Bernanke, Ben (2010), Monetary Policy and the Housing Bubble, Speech prepared for the Annual Meeting of the American Economic Association on January 3.

Bernanke, Ben, Mark Gertler, and Mark Watson (1997), Systematic Monetary Policy and the Effects of Oil Price Shocks, *Brookings Papers of Economic Activity* 1997 (1), 91-157.

Bernanke, Ben, Thomas Laubach, Frederic Mishkin, and Adam Posen (1999), Inflation Targeting: Lessons from the International Experience, Princton University Press.

Bernanke, Ben, and Michael Woodford, (1997), Inflation Targets and Monetary Policy, *Journal of Money, Credit, and Banking* 29 (4), pp. 653-684.

Bharucha, Nargis, and Christopher Kent (1998), Inflation Targeting in a Small Open Economy, Research Discussion Paper 9807, Reserve Bank of Australia.

Blanchard, Olivier J., and Jordi Galí (2007), The Macroeconomic Effects of Oil Price Shocks: Why are the 2000s so Different from the 1970s? NBER Working Paper 13368.

Blanchard, Olivier J., Charles M. Kahn, C. M. (1980), The Solutions Linear Difference Models under Rational Expectations. *Econometrica* 48 (5), pp. 1305-1311.

Brito, Ricardo D., and Brianne Bystedt (2010), The Macroeconomic Effects of Inflation Targeting in Latin-America, *Journal of Development Economics* 91 (2), pp. 198-210.

Buiter, Willem. H. (1982), Predetermined and Non-Predetermined Variables in Rational Expectations Models, *Economics Letter*s 10 (1-2), pp. 49-54.

Bullard, James, Kaushik Mitra (2002), Learning about Monetary Policy Rules, *Journal of Monetary Economics* 29 (6), pp. 1105-1129.

Calvo, Guillermo A. (1983), Staggered Prices in a Utility Maximizing Framework, *Journal of Monetary Economics* 12 (3), pp. 383-398.

Carlstrom, Charles T., and Timothy S. Fuerst (2005), Oil Prices, Monetary Policy, and the Macroeconomy, Federal Reserve Bank of Cleveland, Policy Discussion Paper Number 10.

Clarida, Richard, Jordi Galí, and Mark Gertler (1998), Monetary Policy Rules in Practice: Some International Evidence, *European Economic Review* 42 (6), pp. 1033-1067.

Clarida, Richard, Jordi Galí, and Mark Gertler (2000), Monetary Policy and Macroeconomic Stability: Evidence and Some Theory, *The Quarterly Journal of Economics* 115 (1), pp. 147-166.

Corbo, Vittorio, Oscar Landerrechte, and Klaus Schmidt-Hebbel (2002), Does Inflation Targeting Make a Difference?, in: Loayza, Norman and Raimundo Soto (ed.), Inflation Targeting: Design, Performance, Challenges, pp. 221-269.

Crowe, Christopher (2010), Testing the Transparency Benefits of Inflation Targeting: Evidence from Private Sector Forecasts, *Journal of Monetary Economics* 57 (2), pp. 226-232.

Dovern, Jonas, and Johannes Weisser (2008), Are They Really Rational? – Assessing Professional Macroeconomic Forecasts from the G7-Countries, Kiel Working Paper No. 1447.

Evans, George W. (1989), The Fragility of Sunspot Bubbles. *Journal of Monetary Economics* 23 (2), pp. 297-317.

Evans, George W., Seppo Honkapohja (1992), On the Robustness of Bubbles in Linear RE Models, *International Economic Review* 37 (1), pp. 1-14.

Evans, George W., Seppo Honkapohja (2001), Learning and Expectations in Macroeconomics, Princton University Press, Princton, New Jersey.

Evans, George W., Seppo Honkapohja (2009), Learning and Macroeconomics, *Annual Review of Economics* 1 (1), pp. 421-449.

Farmer, Roger E. A. (1999), The Macroeconomics of Self-Fulfilling Prophecies, MIT Press, Cambridge.

Friedman, Milton (1961), The Lag in Effect of Monetary Policy, *Journal of Political Economy* 69 (5), pp. 447-466.

Galí, Jordi. (2008), Monetary Policy Inflation, and the Business Cycle: An Introduction to the New Keynesian Framework, Princton University Press, Princton, New Jersey.

George, E., King, M., Clementi, D., Budd, A., Buiter, W., Goodhart, C., Julius, D., Plenderleith, I. and J. Vickers (1999), The transmission mechanism of monetary policy, Bank of England.

Gorter, Janko, Jan Jacobs, and Jakob de Haan (2008), Taylor Rules for the ECB using Expectations Data, *Scandinavian Journal of Economics* 110 (3), pp. 473-488.

Hamilton, James D. (1983), Oil and the Macroeconomy since World War II, *Journal of Political Economy* 91 (2), 228248.

Hamilton, James. D., and Ana M. Herrera (2004), Oil Shocks and Aggregate Macroeconomic Behavior: The Role of Monetary Policy, *Journal of Money, Credit and Banking* 36 (2), 265-286.

Heppke-Falk, Kerstin, and Felix Huefner (2004), Expected Budget Deficits and Interest Rate Swap Spreads - Evidence for France, Germany and Italy, Deutsche Bundesbank Discussion Paper No. 40/2004.

Ireland, Peter N. (2007), Changes in the Federal Reserve's Inflation Target: Causes and Consequences, *Journal of Money, Credit and Banking* 39 (8), pp. 1851-1882.

Keynes, John. M. (1936), The General Theory of Employment, Interest and Money, Macmillan Cambridge University Press, Cambridge.

Kilian, Lutz (2009), Not All Oil Price Shocks Are Alike: Disentangling Demand and Supply Shocks in the Crude Oil Market, *American Economic Review* 99 (3), 1053-1069.

Landerrechte, Oscar, Vittorio Corbo, and Klaus Schmidt-Hebbel (2001), Does Inflation Targeting make a Difference?, Central Bank of Chile Working Paper No. 106.

Leigh, Daniel (2008), Estimating the Federal Reserve's Implicit Inflation Target: A State Space Approach, *Journal of Economic Dynamics and Control* 32 (6) , pp. 2013-2030.

Levin, Andrew T., Volker Wieland, and John C. Williams (1999), Robustness of Simple Monetary Policy Rules under Model Uncertainty, in: Taylor, John B. (ed.), Monetary Policy Rules, University of Chicago Press.

Levin, Andrew T., Wieland, Volker and Williams, John C. (2003), The Performance of Forecast-Based Monetary Policy Rules Under Model Uncertainty, *American Economic Review* 93 (3), pp. 622-645.

Lucas, Robert. E. Jr. (1976), Econometric Policy Evaluation: A Critique, in: Brunner, Karl and Allan H. Metzler (eds.) , The Phillips Curve and Labor Markets. Carnegie Rochester Conference Series on Public Policy, vol. 1, Amsterdam, North Holland.

Marcet, Albert , Sargent, Thomas J. (1989), Convergence of Least Squares Learning Mechanisms In Self-Referential Linear Stochastic Models, *Journal of Economic Theory* 48 (2), pp. 337-368.

McCallum, Bennet T. (1983), On Non-Uniqueness on Rational Expectation Models: An Attempt at Perspective, *Journal of Monetary Economics* 11 (2), pp. 139-168.

McCallum, Bennett T. and Nelson, Edward (1999), Performance of Operational Policy Rules in an Estimated Semi-Classical Structural Model, in: Taylor, John B. (ed.), Monetary Policy Rules, University of Chicago Press.

Mehrotra, Aaron, and José R. Sánchez-Fung (2009), Assessing McCallum and Taylor Rules in a Cross-Section of Emerging Market Economies, Bank of Finland, BOFIT Discussion Paper No. 23/2009.

Mishkin, Frederic S., and Klaus Schmidt-Hebbel (2006), Does Inflation Targeting make a difference?, Central Bank of Chile Working Paper No. 404.

Montoro, Carlos (2010), Oil Shocks and Optimal Monetary Policy, *Macroeconomic Dynamics, forthcoming.*

Muth, John F. (1961), Rational Expectations and the Theory of Price Movements, *Econometrica* 29 (3), pp. 315-335.

Natal, Jean-Marc, (2009), Monetary Policy Response to Oil Price Shocks, Federal Reserve Bank of San Francisco, Working Paper 2009-16.

Newey, Whitney K., and Kenneth D. West (1987), A Simple, Positive Semi-Definite, Heteroskedasticity and Autocorrelation Consistent Covariance Matrix, *Econometrica* 55 (3), pp. 703-708.

Orphanides, Anthanasios (2001), Monetary Policy Rules based on Real-Time Data, *The American Economic Review* 91 (4), pp. 964-985.

Orphanides, Anthanasios (2003), Historical Monetary Policy Analysis and the Taylor Rule, *Journal of Monetary Economics* 50 (5), pp. 983-1022.

Österholm, Par (2005), The Taylor Rule: A Spurious Regression, *Bulletin of Economic Research* 57(3), pp. 217-247.

Ravn, Morten, and Harald Uhlig (2002), On Adjusting the Hodrick-Prescott Filter for the Frequency of Observations, *The Review of Economics and Statistics*, 84 (2), pp. 371-375.

Roger, Scott (2009), Inflation Targeting at 20: Achievements and Challanges, IMF Working Paper No. 09/236.

Rudebusch, Glenn D. (2006), Monetary Policy Inertia - Fact or Fiction?, *International Journal of Central Banking* 2, pp. 85-135.

Rülke, Jan-Christoph (2009), Expectations in Financial Markets – A Survey Data Approach, Peter Lang, Frankfurt am Main.

Stone, Mark R., Scott Roger, Anna Nordstrom, Seiichi Shimizu, Turgut Kisinbay, and Jorge Restrepo (2009), The Role of the Exchange Rate in Inflation-Targeting Emerging Market Economies, IMF Occasional Paper No. 267.

Svensson, Lars E. O. (1997), Inflation Forecast Targeting: Implementing and Monitoring Inflation Targets, *European Economic Review* 41 (6), pp. 1111-1146.

Svensson, Lars E. O. (2000), Open-Economy Inflation Targeting, *Journal of International Economics* 50 (1), pp. 155-183.

Svensson, Lars E. O. (2003), What is Wrong with Taylor Rules? Using Judgment in Monetary Policy through Targeting Rules, *Journal of Economic Literature* 41 (2), pp. 427-477.

Svensson, Lars E. O. (2006), Monetary-Policy Challanges: Monetary-Policy Responses to Oil-Price Changes, MIMEO.

Sydsaeter, Knut, Peter Hammond, Atle Seierstad, Arne Strom (2005), Further Mathematics for Economic Analysis, Pearson, Essex.

Taylor, John B. (1993), Discretion versus Policy Rules in Practice, Carnegie-Rochester Conference Series on Public Policy 39, pp. 195-214.

Taylor, John B. (1999), A Historical Analysis of Monetary Policy Rules, in: Taylor, John B. (ed.), Monetary Policy Rules, University of Chicago Press.

Taylor, John B. (2001), The Role of the Exchange Rate in Monetary-Policy Rules, *American Economic Review*, 95 (2), pp. 263-267.

Taylor, John B. (2007), Housing and Monetary Policy, in: Housing, Housing Finance and Monetary Policy, pp. 463-476, Federal Reserve Bank of Kansas City: Kansas City.

Taylor, John B. and John C. Williams (2010), Simple and Robust Rules for Monetary Policy, NBER Working Papers 15908, National Bureau of Economic Research.

Walras, Marie-Esprit L. (1874), Éléments d'économie pure ou théorie de la richesse sociale, Corbaz, Lausanne.

Woodford, Michael (1999), Optimal Monetary Policy Inertia, NBER Working Paper No. 7261, July.

Woodford, Michael (2003), Interest and Prices. Princton University Press, Princton, New Jersey.

Studien zur internationalen Wirtschaftsforschung

Herausgegeben von Ralf Fendel und André Schmidt

Band   1   Dirk Bleich: Monetary Policy Rules. Empirical Applications Based on Survey Data. 2012.

www.peterlang.de